To Jimmie:

Keep up the good work my brother. Stay Positive and focused and thank you for your service.

America: Birth to Greatness and the Black Man's Contribution

James Edward Gatling

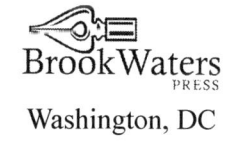

BrookWaters
PRESS

Washington, DC

Published in the United States of America in 2005
Brook Waters Press
P.O. Box 90482
Washington, DC 20090-0482
www.brookwaterspress.com

Copyright © 2005 by Brook Waters Press
Manufacture in the United States
All rights reserved

Library of Congress Cataloging-in-Publication Data
LC Control Number: 2005930164
Text (Book, Microform, Electronic, etc.)
America : birth to greatness and the black man's contribution /
James Edward Gatling; [edited by] Terrence Victor.
1st ed.
Lanham, MD : Brook Waters Press, 2005.
p. cm.
Projected Pub. Date: 0507

First Edition, July 2005

ISBN: 0-9769937-0-8

No part of this book may not be reproduced in any form or by any electronic or mechanical means, including information storage and retrieval systems, without written permission of the publisher.

Printed in the United States of America

Cover Design by Terrence Victor

FIRST EDITION
10 9 8 6 7

Acknowledgement

America Birth to Greatness is a text written to educate and inspire. It is dedicated to my ancestors; for the path that I walk was paved with their blood, sweat, prayers, and tears. It is dedicated to my mother; a strong, kind, beautiful woman who allowed and trusted me to make my own decisions. A walking angel. The most kind and thoughtful person I have ever encountered. It is dedicated *to* my father; the closest friend, *relative motivator,* and role model I had the blessing of having in my life. My father, William P Parker Gatling, died when I was twelve years old, but his love, hard work, and belief in me, adequately prepared me to have the will to succeed. He told me that I was the one. I asked him why? How? Why in these surroundings? He told me "that I must live within my mission for a while to know what I must do". "Son, what you will do for the world will not be for you. That is why you are the one". I haven't had nor needed any mentor, role model, or father-figure since his death. I miss him as much as I would miss the very air I breath.

To my beautiful wife Rachelle and two great sons Julian and Darryl. I could not live without them. To my wife's parents; her father, the late Cal T. Robinson, a good man and father to his family, and my friend, and *her* mother, Mary Robinson, a strong, dedicated mother and wife. Acknowledgements to my brother William "Smiley," and sisters Lou Ann, Angela, Alice, and Ruth and all of my beautiful neices and nephews. Special acknowledgement to all of my nieces, nephews and 21 god-children and to my Aunt Ella Hawkins and my family in New York, Philadelphia, and North Carolina

Special acknowledgements to Pro-Health International and Dr. Iko Ibanga and The Leon H. Sullivan Foundation. Special acknowledgements to Magic Johnson, Steadman Graham, and The Honorable Dr. Benjamin Hooks. I appreciate your friendship and your work and commitment. I acknowledge and thank each and every teacher, instructor, and professor that I have ever had; special thanks to Dean Franklin Powell of Friendship College and Professor Lanny Bowers in Tennessee. Special thanks to Pat Gray, my efficient and priceless personal assistant. I Acknowledge and give Special Thanks to God. God made the difference. God is the difference I express a special appreciation for the numerous children, students, and youth who accepted my love, counseling, motivating, and often **Brainwashing.** I thank you for allowing me into your lives; allowing me into your minds. Thank you for allowing me to turn on that bright light bulb. For the sake of the children I have stood always and still today; and I say to the children of Africa, India, and South America, "I Am On My Way". This I Promise. I live for the children, and will ultimately die for *the* children. May God Bless and Have Mercy On Us All.

Preface

If one were to take a truly spiritual, realistic, and intellectual look at The United States of America and its vastly pluralistic society (the best worldwide) and its magnificent growth and development as a model of the basic building a sovereign nation through democracy. Who knew that the most demoralizing mark on the United States of America that of Slavery would provide great gifts and enlightenment to the world? Why would I state that the enslavement of the Negro captured and/or traded/sold into slavery in America was part of God's larger plan for the evolving of humanity?

The role and participation of the Negro; or African American to use today's terminology, in the development and progressive growth of the United States and the planet is documented and acknowledged to a great extends. The purpose of this book is not to dwell on the many contributions made to America and the global community by Africans but to address the greater, much greater challenge to African-Americans right now and for the times forthcoming. I do not possess specific knowledge on the ships, time, place, and date of the arrival of my ancestors to the United States (The New Land; at that time) or the specific names of my ancestors/forefathers. However, what I do know is that they were no different; no better, no worse; no richer, no poorer then other cultures of people that came to North America. The only indigenous race to the North American continent was the Native Americans (know at that time as "Indians") and Eskimos. Our purpose is also not to dwell on the mistakes of America due to the seeking of growth, expansion, and exploration through the use, abuse, and exploitation of other cultures and concepts of life.

Our purpose here is to take a look at God's plan in direct relation to African-Americans being in America at the present time. We know the Who, the What, the When, the How; but do we truly know the **WHY?** Why were Africans brought to America for enslavement for the foundation and perpetuation of capitalism? Why did some of our own people in Africa sold us to slavery for what they perceived as personal and/or tribal gain? Why the emancipation of Black America only began in 1863 but the realization has yet to commence? Where are African-Americans in God's plan for this beautiful world? Yes it is still and will continue to be a beautiful world, due to the existence and presence of the children. And what we teach them. The vision of a beautiful world that we give them.

Some of the greatest gifts to the progress and evolvement of man and humanity has come as a result of the African-American. The technological advancements as well as those in science, medicine, music, art, and literature are unprecedented. The segment of tragic; yet spiritual irony is that slavery is the actual core of the growth of a nation and evolution of a world.

Dr. Martin Luther King, Jr. was one the few leaders in the history of the world to encompass the words of great men as well the word of God and make them clearly understandable by all. Malcolm X was engulfed with the hatred of white men until a pilgrimage to Mecca enlightened his thinking and concepts and view of religion; praying and praising God with Muslims of all colors, including whites. Malcolm's attempts to communicate this enlightenment to the Muslim community and the world resulted in his assassination. African Americans have a challenge to fulfill. W.E.B. DuBois, Dr. Martin Luther King, Jr., Malcolm X, Huey Newton and the Black Panthers, and Marcus Garvey all had differing ideas on the Black experience and how to address it; however, all had validity.

The mission of this book is to awaken the spirit of the African American because God has placed you on this Earth and in the United States of America specifically at this point in time and history to do something. The knowledge of family history and African American history must be shared with the children. The children have to know who they are, and why they are where they are. Despite where you presently are economically, geographically, socially, or politically; you are here for a specific purpose. We are found to find another. We are taught to teach another. We are saved to save another. Blacks, Whites, Koreans, Chinese, Jew, Palestine's, Egyptians, Muslims, Buddhist, and Catholics; I Love You and you can't do anything about it.

* * *

Contents

1. THE QUEST FOR CONQUEST 11

2. BIRTH OF A NATION 23

3. THE GOOSE THAT LAID THE GOLDEN EGG 41

4. INVESTMENT IN AMERICA 59

5. NATION DEFINING DECADES 71

6. A PEOPLE ON A MISSION 83

7. A MOVEMENT MISUNDERSTOOD 91

8. THE TASK AT HAND 103

REFERENCES 113

CHAPTER I

THE QUEST FOR CONQUEST

Enslavement; the most cruel and inhumane act to impose on a mortal being. It is indeed an act which humiliates and degrades both the oppressor as much as the oppressed. To live in a new land with a new language after being brought over from your native land, away from your family and culture, against your will, to be beaten into obedience and servitude is simply brutal. Surviving within the context of slavery and adapting to its inhumanity and maintaining hope and dignity is amazing. Overcoming slavery and its inhumanity was divine. To contribute to the birth, growth, and success of a nation which is the most dominant nation on the planet with only 227 years since its independence is tremendous. Slavery is the biggest crime ever committed by the United States of America in its entire history. Yet conversely, this may be its greatest benefactor. Slavery was a great tragedy for the Negro, but of great benefit to America and the world.

The Negro contribution and investment in America through work, toil, sacrifice, invention and innovation; transforming and progressing within a system of oppression and utilizing the system as a platform for success. The format of the United States provides a platform for success, manifested through opportunity, access to a chance, freedom of intellect and speech, freedom of expression, creation, and invention. These freedoms help to move a society closer to a more cooperative society; one society, one community, a Community of Will. We have to work to reach this beautiful and righteous goal. However, the format of America provides through the aforementioned freedoms and its constant pursuit to pioneer and discover, a platform; if you will, a stage to present ideas, creations, and innovations that is like no other nation.

Would the ideas and innovations of Dr. Charles Richard Drew, which revolutionized the field of medicine; creator of the concept and the implementation of a Blood Bank, have been globally embraced and utilized if he were born, raised, researched and discovered this tremendous medical breakthrough from Kenya, Africa? Would the Multiple Effect Vacuum Sugar Evaporator, a device invented by Norbert Rillieux, which revolutionized sugar processing been so widely received if he were born and discovered it in Sudan? Further do you think he could have even received recognition for such an invention? It is funny how great an Individual, a Community, a Nation can become when they are allowed to evolve freely. To evolve freely; independent of interference or rule from foreign nations and interests. Evolve free of man's quest for dominance and control over other men, nations, and civilizations. Man's quest for power and control over other men and their lives and progress is not exclusive to any continent or period of time in world history. The forcing of a man into a powerless and hopelessly dependent position and community. Forcing man into a "Community of Obedience."

The primitive civilizations were "Communities of Obedience;" which obedience to God-Kings or Kings under God were their cement over the ruled. The Nomadic tendency, on the other hand, has always been towards a different type of association; a "Community of Will." In a wandering, fighting community the individual must be self-reliant and disciplined. The leaders of such communities must be leaders who are followed, not masters who compel. This *"Community of Will"* is traceable throughout the entire history of mankind; everywhere we find in the original disposition of all the Nomads alike, Nordic, Semitic, or Mongolian. As the history of man has developed he has experienced the appearance of new and complicating elements in the story of human societies. We have seen transitions of politics, people, governments, and societies. But, in spite of all such complications, the broad antagonism between the Method of Obedience and the Method of Will runs through history into our current times. To this very day their reconciliation remains incomplete.

Civilization even and is most servile forms has always offered much that is enormously attractive and congenial to mankind; but something restless and untamed in our races that strive continually to convert civilization from its original reliance upon not participating obedience into a community of participating wills. It is a community of positive and unified participation of will that is successful and self-reliant. This natural, this temperamental struggle of mankind to reconcile civilization with freedom has been kept alive age after age by the military and political means of every Community of Obedience that has ever existed. Understand that once men are broken into obedience, it can be very easily captured and transferred. This fact has presented itself a number of times; from the early history of Egypt, Mesopotamia, and India to the 20th Century Times of Zaire, Russia, and Korea; and the people being passed from one lordship to another. A servile community or civilization is a standing invitation to predatory free men. However, or the other hand, a Community of Will necessitates a synergy of intractable factors. Thus, it is a far harder community to bring about, and yet, more difficult to maintain. But; once established, impossible to defeat.

The battle of the Community of Obedience vs. The Community of Will continues today as in all of history. The battle for first position; yet, conversely, the answer lies in the middle of the spheres. The ideal government which should be strived for is one which embodies the modern ideal of a worldwide educational government, in which the ordinary man's neither the slave of an absolute monarch nor a demagogue-ruled state, but an informed, inspired, and consulted part of the larger community. It is upon the term and implementation of the term "educational" which the solid foundation of inter-community cooperative spirit and growth is based, and upon this ideal that information must precede consultation. It is in the practical realization of this data, that education is a collective function and not a private affair, that one essential distinction of the "Modern State" from any of its precursors lies.

In modern society, men are coming to realize on a larger scale that they must be informed first and then consulted. Before an individual can effectively vote, one must hear the evidence. Before one can decide, one must know. It is not by setting up polling booths, but by setting up schools and making literature, culture, knowledge, and news universally assessable. This is the way the people are raised from servitude and confusion to that willingly cooperative state which is the modern ideal. Votes, in themselves are a worthless thing. Men had votes in Italy in the time of the Gracchi. Their votes did not help them. Until a man has education, a vote is a useless and dangerous thing for him to possess. The ideal community, of which, we should constantly strive to gravitate to is not simply a Community of Will. It is a Community of Knowledge and Will, replacing a Community of adherence and blind obedience. Education is the adapter which will make the Nomadic spirit of freedom and self-reliance compatible with cooperation's which facilitates the wealth and security of civilization. This is indeed a great mission to undertake. The United States is the only nation on the planet at present where this can take place. The question is; will the powers that be allow this to take place?. Can we let it be?.

The United States of America is the most vastly pluralistic society on our planet, with rights and freedoms and opportunities for its citizens unlike any nation on any continent; worldwide. These "rights" that I address are rooted in the very Constitution of the United States of America and its Amendments to the Constitution to facilitate the establishment, acceptance and adherence to these rights. However, as a society, we must facilitate education to guarantee destined for of historical greatness and ultimate effectiveness. What is quite intriguing is the "discovery", birth, growth, and success of these United States of America and its ability to exist, endure and dominate. It is widely known that the "discovery" of America was not the intended plan of Christopher Columbus and was to a large extent accidental; at lease from a geographical standpoint. He must be given credit for answering the questions with regard to the world and it's circumference and achieving his ultimate goal, To Prove That The World Was Round. However the "Discovery" or "Birth" of America, if you will, was destined despite geography or the intentions of man. For intellectual and educational purposes, and with relation to our text and the history of America, Mr. Columbus and his contribution merit acknowledgment as well discussion and even debate.

In 1486 a Portuguese by the name of Bartolomeo Diaz, reported that he had rounded the South of Africa. So opened the way for the great enterprise of Vasco de Gama, 11 years later. The Portuguese were already working their way to the East before the Spanish went West. A certain Genoese, Christopher Columbus, began to think more and more of what is now very obvious and needs no natural intellectual undertaking, but what strained the imagination of the 15th century to the utmost; a voyage due West across the Atlantic. At this time nobody knew of the existence of North America as a separate continent. Columbus strongly believed that the world was a sphere, but he underestimated its size. The travels of Marco Polo had given Columbus and exaggerated idea of the extent of Asia, and he supposed therefore, that Japan, with his reputation for great wealth of gold, lay across the Atlantic in about the global position of Mexico. Columbus had made various voyages in the Atlantic; he had been to Iceland and perhaps heard of Vinland, which must have greatly encouraged these ideas of his. This project of literally sailing into the sunset became the dominating purpose of his life.

Columbus was a penniless man, some accounts of history say that he was bankrupt, and his only way of securing a ship was to get someone to entrust him with a command. He went first to King John II of Portugal, who listened to him,

THE QUEST FOR CONQUEST

made difficulties and then arranged for an expedition to start without his knowledge, to facilitate a purely Portuguese expedition. This highly diplomatic attempt to steal and launch an expedition without the conceiving man failed horribly. The crew became mutinous, the captain lost heart and returned home (1483). Columbus then went the Royal Court of Spain. At first he could get no ship, crew, nor powers. Spain was assailing Granada, the last foothold of the Moslems in Western Europe. Most of Spain was recovered by the Christians between the 11th and the 13th centuries; then had a pause; and now all Christian Spain, united by the marriage of Ferdinand of Aragon and Isabella of Castelle, was settling itself to the completion of the Christian conquest. Despairing of Spanish help, Columbus sent his brother Bartolomew to Henry VII of England, but the adventure did not attract the canny Monarch. Finally in 1492, Granada fell; some slight compensation for the Christian loss of Constantinople 50 years before; and then helped by the merchants of the town of Palos, Columbus got his ships. Three ships, of which only one, the Santa Maria, of 100 tons strong, was decked. The other two were open boats of half that weight. The expedition; numbered altogether 88 men went South to the Canary Islands and then stood out across the unknown seas, in beautiful weather and a helpful wind.

The story of that momentous voyage of two months and nine days must be told in detail to be truly appreciated. The crew were full of doubts and fears that they might have sailed on forever. They were comforted by seeing some birds, later finding a pole worked with tools, and a branch with strange berries. At 10:00 P.M. on the night of October 11, 1492 Columbus saw a light ahead. The next morning land was sighted, and it was early in the day when Columbus landed on the shores of the New World; richly apparelled and bearing the Royal Banner of Spain. Early in 1493 Columbus returned to Europe. He brought gold, cotton, strange beasts and birds and two wild-eyed painted Indians to be baptized. He had not found Japan. He thought that he reached and discovered India. The Islands he "discovered" were therefore called, "The West Indies." The same year he sailed again with a great expedition of 17 ships and 1,500 men, with the expressed permission of the Pope to take possession of these new lands for the Spanish Crown. I cannot address his experiences as Governor of this Spanish colony, nor how he was superseded and put in chains by a swarm of Spanish adventurers exploring the new lands. But what is interesting to note is that Columbus died ignorant of the fact that he discovered a new continent. He believed to the day of his death that he had sailed around the world to Asia. The news of his discoveries caused great excitement through Western Europe.

It spurred the Portuguese to renewed attempts to reach India by the South

African route. In 1519 a Portuguese sailor, Ferdinand Magellan, under the employment of the Spanish King, coasted to the Americas', passed through the dark and forbidden "*Strait of Magellan*", and came into the Pacific Ocean, which had already been sighted by Spanish explorers who had crossed the Isthmus of Panama.

Magellan's expedition continued across the Pacific Ocean Westward. This was a fall more heroic voyage than that of Columbus; for 89 days Magellan sailed unflinchingly across the vast, empty ocean, citing nothing but two small desert Islands. The crews were rotten with scurvy; there was little water, and putrid biscuits to eat. Rats were hunted eagerly; cowhide was gnawed and sawdust eaten to fight the pangs of hunger. In this condition the expedition reached the Ladrones. They discovered the Philippines, and here Magellan was killed in a fight with the natives. Several of Magellan's captains were murdered. Five ships had started with Magellan in August 1519 with 280 men; in July 1522, the Victoria, with a remnant of 130 men aboard, returned up the Atlantic to her anchorage near the Mole of Seville, in the River Guadalquivir -- the first ship that ever circumnavigated the planet.

The English, Dutch, and French nations came rather late to exploration. And when they did come in, their first efforts were directed to sailing around the North of America as Magellan had sailed around the South, and then to sailing around the North of Asia as Vasco da Gama had sailed around the South of Africa. Both expeditions were unsuccessful. In America and in the East, Spain and Portugal had half a century's start on England, France, and Holland. Germany never started. The King of Spain was Emperor of Germany in those crucial years, and the Pope had given the monopoly of America to Spain, and not simply to Spain but to the Kingdom of Castile. This must have restrained both Germany and Holland at first from American expeditions; for their towns were Quasi-Independent without Monarchs and organized enough for oceanic exploration. Slowly throughout the 16th century the immense good fortune of Castile unfolded itself before the dazzled eyes of Europe. She found a new world, abounding in gold and silver and wonderful possibilities of settlement. It was all hers, because the Pope said so. The court of Rome, in an access of magnificence, had divided this new world of strange lands; which was now open to the European imagination, between the Spanish, who were to have everything West of an line 370 Leagues West of the Cape Verde Islands, and the Portuguese, to whom everything East of this line was given. At first the people encountered by the Spaniards in America were said to be "savages" of a Mongoloid type. Many of these savages were cannibals.

THE QUEST FOR CONQUEST

It is a misfortune for science that the first Europeans to reach America were these rather incurious Spaniards, without any scientific passion, thirsty for gold, and full of blind bigotry from a recent religious war. They made few intelligent observations of the native methods and ideas of these "different" people. They slaughtered them, they robbed them, they enslaved them, and they baptized them; they made little note if any to the customs and culture which changed and vanished under their assault. As the Spaniards penetrated into the continent, they found and they attacked, plundered, and destroyed two separate civilized systems that had developed in America, perhaps independently of the civilized systems of the old world.

One of them was the alter civilization of Mexico; the other, that of Peru. They were said to have arisen out of the Neolithic sub-civilization that had spread across the Pacific, Island by Island, step by step, age after age, from its region of origin round and about the Mediterranean. The Spaniards ill-treated the natives, they quarrelled among themselves; the law and order of Spain were months and years away from them; it was very slowly that the phase of violence and conquest passed into a phase of government and settlement. But long before there was much order in America, a steady stream of gold and silver began to flow across the Atlantic to the Spanish Government and people. After the first violent treasure hunt came plantations and the working of mines. With that arose the first labor difficulty in the new world. Indians were enslaved with much brutality and injustice; but to the honor of the Spaniards this was greatly criticized. The importation of African Slaves from West Africa began quite early in the 16th Century. After some retrogression, Mexico, Brazil, and South America began to develop into great slave-holding, wealth-producing lands.

So it was that Spain rose to temporary power and prominence in the World's affairs. It was a very sudden and quite memorable rise. Since the 11th Century this fertile and corrugated peninsula had been divided against itself, its Christian population had sustained a perpetual conflict with the Moors; then by what seems like an accident it achieved unity just in time to reap the first harvest of benefit from the discovery of America. Before that time Spain had always been a poor country; its only wealth was in its mines. For a century, however, through its monopoly of the gold and silver of America, it dominated the world. The discovery of the huge continent of America; thinly inhabited, undeveloped, and admirably adapted for European settlement and exploration. The simultaneous discovery of great areas of unworked country South of the torrid equatorial regions of Africa that had hither to limited European knowledge, and the gradual realization of vast Island regions in the Eastern seas; as yet untouched by Western Civilization, was a presentation of opportunity to mankind unprecedented in all of history. It was as if the people of Europe had come into some splendid legacy. Their world had suddenly quadrupled. There was more than enough for all; they had only to take these lands and continue to do well by them, and their crowded poverty would vanish like a dream. They received this glorious legacy like ill-bred heirs; it meant no more to them than a fresh occasion for atrocious disputes. But what community of human beings has ever preferred creation to conspiracy? What nation in the history of the world has ever worked with another when it contrived to do that other than injure or eliminate? The powers of Europe began by a frantic claiming of new realms. They went into exhausting conflicts. Spain, who claimed first and most, and who was for a time mistress of two-thirds of America, made no better use of her possession than to bleed herself to death therein.

History tells how the Papacy in its assertion of world dominion, instead of maintaining the common duty of the Catholic Church to make a great common civilization in the new lands, divided the American continent between Spain and Portugal. This naturally roused the hostility of the excluded nations. The seamen of England showed no respect for either claim, and set themselves particularly against the Spanish; the Swedish turned their Protestantism to a similar account. The Hollanders as well as his most Catholic Majesty of France hesitated; but then all of these powers were soon busy staking out claims in North America and the West Indies. The Danish (which at that time included Norway and Iceland) and the Hollanders, also with the French monarchy under Cardinal Richelieu and under Louis XIV eating its way across the Spanish Netherlands towards their frontier, did not have the undistracted resources of Great Britain to fully and freely invest in overseas undertakings and adventures. Further, the absolutist efforts of James I and Charles I, and the restoration of Charles II, had the effect of driving out from England a great number of sturdy-minded, republican-spirited men. Men of substance and of basic character, who set up in America, particularly in New England, out of reach, as they thought, of the King and his taxes.

The Mayflower was only one of the pioneer vessels of a stream of emigrants and slaves. It was to Britain's advantage that they remained, though dissentient in spirit, still under the British flag. The Dutch never sent out settlers of the same quantity and quality, first because the Spanish rulers would not let them; and secondly because Spain had not gotten possession of their own country; that they supposedly discovered. Thus, the Dutch settlements, along with the Swedish and the French, also succumbed to Britain; New Amsterdam became British in 1674, and its name changed to New York (which can be found in Washington Irving's Knickerbocker's History of New York). By 1740 the British power was established along the East coast from Savannah, Georgia to the St. Lawrence River, and newfound land and the considerable Northern areas, the Hudson Bay Company territories, had been acquired by treaty from the French.

The British occupied Barbados; almost their oldest American possession in 1605, and acquired Jamaica, the Bahamas, and British Honduras from the Spaniards. While vacationing in Barbados in March 2003, I found not only the strong presence of British influence; but of British control, domination, and rule. I was overwhelmingly happy to see Black people in control of all operations, from the pilots on the planes to the police, politicians, and government. However, the quest for knowledge often in finding wisdom and pain. My driver Jeremy was born and raised in Barbados and educated in the United States at Morgan State University in Baltimore, Maryland. He returned home to help run the family funeral home business. When Jeremy educated me on the socioeconomic, political state, and rule of Barbados in real terms, not of my observations, my sunglasses did their best to shield my tears of the knowledge and the disappointment. In recalling the pain of that experience; I digress. The French were cutting deals, but they were pursuing a very dangerous and alarming game. France had established real settlements in Quebec and Montreal to the North and at New Orleans in the South, and her explorers and agents had pushed North and South, making treaties with the American Indians of the Great Plains and setting up claims across the continent behind the British. Their folly was in their failure to build settlements as they negotiated the treaties. Conversely, the British colonies were being solidly settled by masses of people; they already numbered a population of over one million. The French at that time hardly counted 100,000. Although they had a number of brilliant travelers and missionaries at work, they had no substance in terms of population behind them. War broke out in 1754, and in 1759 the British and Colonial forces under General Wolfe took Quebec and completed the conquest of Canada in 1760. In 1763 Canada was finally ceded to Britain. However, the Western part of the rather infinite region of Louisiana in the South, named after Louis XIV, renamed outside of the British sphere. It was taken over by Spain; and in 1800 it was recovered by France. Finally, in 1803, it was purchased from France by President Thomas Jefferson and the United States Government for $15,000,000.00. What a deal. Further, in the Canadian War the American colonists gained considerable experience in the Art of War; a knowledge of British military organization that would be of great use to the Republic of America shortly thereafter.

For a while Britain and France clashed powers and plans in America; both were advancing their dominance worldwide. India was indeed an interesting settlement of Britain. Initially adventurers and traders and the establishment of the East India Trading Company, which was originally the idea of Queen Elizabeth, was no more than a company of sea adventurers. This trading company, with its tradition of gain, found itself dealing not merely in spices and dyes and tea and jewels; but in the revenues and territories of Princes' and destinies of India. Britain had gone to buy and sell, and found itself achieving a tremendous piracy. There was no one to challenge its proceedings. By 1761, the British found themselves completely dominant in the India Peninsula. However, India's independence was yet to come. At the same time China was in a phase of expansion. The Manchu conquerors had brought a new energy into Chinese affairs, and their Northern interests led to a considerable Northward expansion to the Chinese civilization and influence into Manchuria and Mongolia.

So it was that by the mid 1700's the Russians and Chinese were in contact with Mongolia. At this period China ruled Eastern Turkestan, Tibet, Nepal, Burma, and Annam. Chinese porcelain was the best in the world; perfect for civilized society. There was a steady stream of exploration throughout the century to the Palaces, chateaux's and country houses of the European nobility and gentry. European pottery imitated and competed with the Chinese product but never improved or completely matched it. The European Tea Trade also began at this time. Japan, besides its invasion of Korea and its aggression upon China, Japan was relatively quiet before the 19th century, like China under the Ming Dynasty, Japan had set her face resolutely against the interference of foreigners in their affairs. She was a country leading her own civilized life, magically sealed against intruders China's picture que and romantic history stands apart from the general drama of global or regional human affairs. However, the power and presence of Britain and Europe was ever increasing.

The great geographical discoveries of the 16th century had so enlarged human resources that for all their divisions, for all the waste, of their wars and policies, the people of Europe enjoyed a considerable and increasing prosperity. Central Europe recovered steadily from the devastation of The Thirty Years' War. They expanded their influence and power and continued to benefit from the riches of America. With Slavery flourishing in the southern colonies of America, the free labor force was a mainstay in its economy. In Europe as in America at this time, the poor were oppressed and used for the progression of the landowners and other people of affluence who without doubt influenced political, economic, and social affairs and legislation. What is interesting is that however numerous a downtrodden class may be, and however extreme its miseries, it will never be able to make an effective protest until it achieves solidarity by recognizing or developing

THE QUEST FOR CONQUEST

a Common General Idea. Educated men and women of ideas are more necessary to a popular political movement than to any other political process. A monarchy learns by ruling, and an oligarchy of any type or culture has the education of affairs; the education of opportunity, the education of influence, and the education on the institution of power. However the common man, the peasant or toiler, has no experience in large matters, and can exist politically only through the services, devotion, and guidance of educated men.

This enabled the powers of organization, church, and government of Europe to spread their influence of it's "Great Powers" globally. Those great powers were indeed "flexing," in modern terms. The struggles of the 16th and 17th century Princes' for ascendancies and advantages developed into a more cunning and complicated struggle of foreign offices and domains, masquerading as idealized "great powers," as the 18th century wore on. The intricate and pretentious art of diplomacy developed. The "Prince" ceased to be a single and secretive Machiavellian schemer, and became merely the crowned symbol of a Machiavellian scheme. Prussia, Russia, and Austria fell upon and divided Poland. France was baffled in profound schemes against Spain. Britain circumvented the "Designs of France" in America and acquired Canada, and got the better of France in India. And then a remarkable thing occurred, a thing quite shocking to European diplomacy. The British colonies in America flatly refused to have any further part or lot in this game of "Great Powers". They objected that they had no voice and no great interest in these European schemes and conflicts, and they refused to bear any portion of the burden of taxation that these foreign policies entailed. "Taxation without representation is tyranny". This was their dominant ideal. Of course, this decision to separate did not flush out complete and finished from the American mind at the beginning of these troubles.

In America in the 18th century, just as England in the 17th, there was an entire willingness, indeed a desire on the part of ordinary men to leave foreign affairs in the hands of the King and his Ministers. But there was an equally strong desire on the part of ordinary men to be neither taxed nor interfered within terms of their ordinary lives and pursuits relating thereto. These are incompatible wishes. Common men cannot shirk world politics and at the same time enjoy private freedom; but it has taken countless generations to learn this. The first impulse in the American revolt against the government in Great Britain was, therefore, simply a resentment against the taxation and interference that followed necessarily from "foreign policy," without any clear recognition of what was involved in that objection. It was only when the revolt was consummated that the people of the American Colonies recognized at all that they had repudiated the "great power" view of life. The sentence in which that repudiation was expressed was Washington's injunction to "avoid entangling alliances."

* * *

CHAPTER II

BIRTH OF A NATION

For a full century the United States Colonies of Great Britain in North America; liberated and independent as the United States of America, stood apart altogether from the blood-stained intrigues and conflicts of the European foreign offices. However, they were not the first to stand aloof. Since the Treaty of Westphalia in 1648, the Confederate States of Switzerland, in their mountain fastness, had sustained their right to exclusion from the schemes of Kings and Empires, but in the colonies, a nation was birthed and breathing. History with regard to the colonies reveal that they were initially a mere fringe of population along the Atlantic coast, spreading gradually inland and finding in the Allegheny and Blue Mountains a very serious barrier. Among the oldest of these settlements was the colony of Virginia, the name of which pays homage to Queen Elizabeth, the Virgin Queen of England.

The first expedition found a colony was that by Sir Walter Raleigh in 1584, but there was no permanent settlement at that time, and the beginnings of Virginia date from the foundation of The Virginia Company in 1606, in the reign of James I (1603 - 1625). The story of John Smith and the early founders of Virginia, and how the Indian Princess Pocahontas married one of his gentlemen, is an English and American classic. In growing tobacco the Virginians found the beginning of prosperity. At the same time that the Virginia Company was founded, the Plymouth Company obtained a charter for the settlement of the country to the North of Long

Island South, to which the English laid claim. In 1620 the Northern region began to be New England, which became Connecticut, New Hampshire, Rhode Island, and Massachusetts.

They were men of a different stamp and ideal then that of the people of Virginia; they were Protestants discontented with The Anglican Church Compromise, and republican-spirited men hopeless of resistance to the Grand Monarchy of James I and Charles I. Their pioneer ship was The Mayflower, which founded New Plymouth in 1620. The dominant northern colony was Massachusetts. Differences in religious ideals and methods of toleration (Law & Order) led to the separation of the three other Puritan Colonies from Massachusetts. It illustrates the scale upon which things were done in those days that the entire State of New Hampshire was claimed as belonging to a certain Captain John Mason, and that he offered to sell it to King Charles II in 1671 in exchange for the right to import 300 tons of French wine free of duty; an offer which was refused. The real estate which is now Maine was purchased by Massachusetts from its alleged owner for 1,250 pounds

The English Civil War was more recognized as the great rebellion which ended with the beheading of Charles I on January 30, 1649. New England expressed sympathies for the Parliament, but Virginia was cavalier; and there were 350 miles which separated these settlements and their were no serious hostilities. With the return of the monarchy in 1600, there was a vigorous development of British colonization in America. Charles II and his associates were greedy for gain, and the British Crown had no wish to make any further experiments in illegal taxation at home. But the undefined relations of the colonies to the Crown and the British government seemed to afford promise of financial adventure across the Atlantic. Lord Baltimore had already in 1632 set up a colony that was to be a home of religious freedom for Catholics under the attractive name of Maryland.

To the North and East of Virginia; the Quaker Penn (whose father rendered valuable service to Charles II) established himself to the North of Philadelphia and founded the colony of Pennsylvania. Its main boundary with Maryland and Virginia was delimited by two men, Mason and Dixon, whose "Mason-Dixon Line" was destined to become a very important line in the later affairs of the United States of America. Carolina, which was originally an unsuccessful French Protestant establishment which owes its name not to Charles (Carolus) II of England, but to Charles IX of France, had fallen into English hands and was settled at several points. Between Maryland and New England stretched a number of small Dutch and Swedish settlements, of which the chief town was New Amsterdam. These settlements were captured from the Dutch by the British in 1664, lost again in

BIRTH OF A NATION

1673, and restored by treaty when Holland and England, made peace in 1674. Thereby the whole coast from Maine to Carolina became in some way or other, a British possession.

To the South the Spanish were established; their headquarters were at Fort Saint Augustine in Florida, and in 1733 the town of Savannah was settled by philanthropist Oblethorpe from England, who had taken pity on the miserable people imprisoned for debts in England, and rescued a number of them from prison to become the founders of a new colony, Georgia, which was to be a bulwark against the Spanish. So by the middle of the 18th century there were settlements along the American coastline; the New England group of Puritans and free Protestants- Maine (belonging to Massachusetts), New Hampshire, Connecticut, Rhode Island, and Massachusetts; the Dutch group, which was now divided into New York (New Amsterdam rechristened), New Jersey, and Delaware (Swedish before it was Dutch, and in its earliest British phase attached to Pennsylvania); followed by Catholic Maryland, Cavalier Virginia, Carolina (which was divided into North and South Carolina) and Oglethrope's Georgia. Soon after, a number of Tyrolese Protestants took refuge in Georgia, and there was a considerable immigration of German cultivators into Pennsylvania. Such were the miscellaneous origins of the citizens of the thirteen colonies. The possibility of their ever becoming united would have struck an impartial observer in 1760 as being very slight.

Factor in the initial differences of origin, fresh differences were created by climate. North of the Mason-Dixon Line, farming was practiced mainly as in British or central European fashion by free white cultivators. The settled country of New England took on a likeness to the English countryside, and considerable areas of Pennsylvania developed fields and farm houses like those of South Germany. The distinctive conditions in the North had very important effects socially. Masters and men had to labor together as backwoods men, and were equalized in the process. They did not start equally; many "servants" are mentioned in the roster of the Mayflower, but the platform of America would allow them the venue for freedom. They rapidly became equal under colonial conditions; there was a vast tract of land to be had for the taking, and the "servant" went off and took land like his master. The English class system disappeared. Under colonial conditions there arose equality in the facilities both of body and mind, and an individual independence of judgement impatient of interference from England. However, South of the Mason-Dixon Line tobacco growing began, and the warmer climate encouraged the establishment of plantations with gang labor.

Red Indian captives were tried but found to be too homicidal (independent rebellion); Cromwell sent Irish Prisoners of War to Virginia, which did much to reconcile the Royalist planter's to Republicanism; convicts were sent out, and there was a considerable trade in kidnapped children who were said to being "spirited away" to America to become apprentices or bond slaves. But the most convenient form of gang labor proved to be that of the African Slave, known as Negroes. The first Negro Slaves were brought to Jamestown, Virginia by a Dutch ship as early as 1620. By 1700 Negro Slaves were scattered all over the states, but Virginia, Maryland, and the Carolinas were their chief regions of employment, and while the communities to the North were communities of not very rich and very poor working farming men, the South developed a type of large proprietor and a white community of overseers and professional men subsisting and essentially surviving on slave labor.

Slave labor was a necessity to the social and economic system that had grown up in the South; yet, in the North the presence of slaves and slavery were unnecessary and inconvenient. Conscientious scruples about slavery were more free; therefore, free to develop and flourish in the Southern atmosphere. The North looked down upon slavery, as it flourished in the South. This was a major factor in the heterogeneous mixture of the British colonies. However, if the inhabitants of the thirteen colonies were miscellaneous in their origins and various in their habits and sympathies, they had three very strong antagonisms in common. They had a common interest against the Red Indians. For a time they shared a common dread of French conquest and dominion. And thirdly, they were all in conflict with the claims of the British Crown and the commercial secretness of the narrow oligarchy who dominated the British Parliament and British affairs. And as far as the first danger went, the Indians were a constant adversary but never more than a threat of disaster. They remained divided against themselves, yet they exhibited the possibilities of unity upon a larger scale.

The Five Nations of the Iroquois (1760) were a very important league of tribes. But it never succeeded in playing off the French against the English to secure itself, and no Red Indian Genghis Khan ever arose among these Nomads of the new world. The French aggression was a more serious threat. The French never established settlements in America on a scale to compete with the English, but their government set about the encirclement of the colonies and their subjugation in a terrifying systematic manner. The English in America were colonist; the French were explorers, adventurers, agents, missionaries, merchants, and soldiers. Only in Canada did they strike root. French statesmen sat over maps and dreamed dreams, and established Forts Southward from the Great Lakes and Northward up the Mississippi River and the Ohio River. The struggle of France and Britain

BIRTH OF A NATION

was a worldwide struggle. It was decided in India, in Germany, and on the high seas. In the peace treaty of Paris in 1763, the French gave England Canada, and relinquished Louisiana to the inert hands of declining Spain. It was the complete abandonment of America by France. The lifting of the French danger left the colonists unencumbered to face their third common antagonist; the Crown and Government of their motherland.

It is interesting how the governing class of Great Britain steadily acquired the land and destroyed the liberty of common people throughout the 18th century, and how greedily and blindly the Industrial Revolution; which forever changed the fundamental importance of human economics, was brought about. The importance of the Industrial Revolution lies in its effect on the dynamics of human relations because it opened a great gulf between employer and the employed. In the past every manufacturing worker had the hope of becoming an independent master. Even the slave craftsman in Babylon and Rome were protected by laws that enabled the slave to save and purchase their freedom and set up shop for themselves. But now a factory and its engines and machines became a vast and costly thing measured by its effect on the common man's pocket. As a student of Economics and of History, I submit to you that the Industrial Revolution was the true birth and arrival of capitalism. The reduction of operational expenses thru mass production. Wealthy men had come together to create an enterprise, credit, and facilities; that is to state in today's terminology, "capital" was required. Setting up shop for oneself ceased to be a normal hope and goal for the common man. The worker as henceforth a worker from the cradle to the grave. Present day, the United States of America is one of the countries in the world where this is not true.

Although powerful, the British Parliament, through the decay of the representative methods of the House of Commons, had become both in its upper and lower houses merely the instrument of government through the big landowners. Both the wealthy property holders and Great Britain were deeply interested in America; the former as private adventurers; the latter partly as representing the speculative exploitations of the Stuart Kings, and partly as representing the State in search of funds for the expense of foreign policy. Neither Lords nor Crown were disposed to regard the traders, planters, and common people of the colonies with any more consideration than they did the Yeomen and small cultivators at home. At the bottom of the priority list were the interests of the common man in Great Britain, Ireland, and America, which were the same. Each were being squeezed by the same system. But while in Britain oppressor and the oppressed were closely tangled in one intimate social system; in America the Crown and the exploiter were far away, and men could not get together and develop a sense of community against their common enemy. Further, the American colonies had the important advantage of possessing a separate and legal origin of resistance to the British Government in the assembly or legislature of her colony that was necessary for the management of local affairs. The common man in Britain, cheated out of his proper representation in the Commons, had no organ, no center of expression or action for his discontents.

Despite the variety of concepts, beliefs, and practices of the colonies, they recognized and shared the same oppression and grievances. These grievances fell under three main areas: attempts to secure for British adventurers or the British government the profits of exploitation of the new lands, systematic restrictions upon trade designed to keep the foreign trade of the colonies entirely in British hands, so that the colonial exports all went through Britain and only British made goods were to be used in America; and finally, attempts at taxation through the British Parliament as the supreme taxing authority of the empire. Under the pressure of this triple system of annoyances the American colonists were forced to do a very considerable amount of hard political thinking. Such men as Patrick Henry and James Otis began to discuss the fundamental ideas of government and political association very much as they had been discussed in England in the great days of Cromwell's Commonwealth. They began to deny both the divine origin of Kings and the supremacy of the British Parliament James Otis wrote:

"God made all men naturally equal. Ideas of Earthly superiority are educational, not innate. Kings were made for the good of the people, and not the people for Kings. No Government has a right to make slaves of its subjects. Though most Governments are "de facto" arbitrary, and consequently the curse and scandal of human nature, yet none are "de jure" arbitrary."

It is ironic that with the such eloquent words of fairness and acknowledgment of natural human rights expressed by the American colonists; they were ignoring their own acts of oppression. The colonists either participated, exploited, benefited, prospered, argued, observed, or ignored the oppression and outright inhumanity of slavery in the American Colonies. This ferment in the political ideals are the Americans was started by English leaven. The most influential English writer was John Locke (1632-1704), whose Treaties on Civil Government may be taken, as much as one single book can be taken in such cases, as the point of departure for the modern democratic ideas, theories, and concepts. But Men do not begin to act upon theories. It is always some real danger, some practical necessity, which produces a new and perplexing state of affairs that theory comes to its own.

BIRTH OF A NATION

It is at that time that theory is put to the test. The discord of interest and ideas between the colonists was brought to a fighting issue by the obstinate resolve of the British Parliament after the peace of 1763 to impose taxation upon the American colonists.

Britain was at peace and flushed with successes; it seemed an admirable opportunity to settling old accounts with these recalcitrant colonists. However, the great British property owners found a power beside themselves, of much the same mind as them, but a little divergent in its ends: the reviving Crown. King George III, who had begun his reign in 1760, was resolved to be much more of a King than his two German predecessors. He could speak English; he claimed to "Glory in the name of Britain;" and indeed, it is not a bad name for a man with the scarcity trace of English, Welsh, or Scottish blood in his veins. In the American colonies and overseas possessions generally, with their indefinite charters or no charters at all, it seemed to him that the Crown might claim authority and obtain resources and powers absolutely denied to it by the strong and jealous aristocracy in Britain. This inclined many of the rich nobleman to a sympathy for the colonist that they might not otherwise have shown. What is interesting here is that they had no objection to the exploitation of the colonies in the interest of the British "Private Enterprise;" yet they had very strong objections to the strengthening of the Crown by the exploitation so as to then make it independent of themselves.

The war that broke out was, therefore, in reality not a war of Britain and the American colonists, it was a war between the British government and the American colonists, with a body of nobleman and a considerable amount of public feeling in England on the side of the latter. An earlier move in 1764 was an attempt to raise revenue for Britain in the colonies by requiring that newspapers and documents of various sorts should be stamped. This was stiffly resisted, the British Crown was shocked, confused, and unprepared for this outright defiance. Thus, The Stamp Act were repealed. The repeal was greeted by riotous celebrations in London. In fact, more hearty and riotous than those in the colonies. But the Stamp Act affair was only an entrée and a turbulent stream flowing towards war. Upon a score of pretexts, and up and down the coast, the representatives of the British government were busy asserting their authority and making British government intolerable. The quartering of soldiers upon the colonists was a great nuisance. Rhode Island was particularly active in defying the trade restrictions. The Rhode Islanders were "free traders," that is to say; smugglers. In 1773, with a total disregard of the existing colonial tea trade, special advantages for the importation of tea into America were given by the British Parliament to the East India Company. It was resolved by the colonists to refuse and boycott this tea. When the tea importers in Boston showed themselves resolute to land their cargo's; on December 16, 1773 a band of men disguised as Indians, in the presence of a great crowd of people, boarded the three ships and threw the tea overboard.

All of 1774 was occupied with the gathering of resources on both sides for the forthcoming conflict. It was decided by the British Parliament in the Spring of 1774 to punish Boston by closing her port. Boston's port trade was to be destroyed unless she accepted that tea. It was a quite typical instance of that silly "firmness" which shatters Empires. In order to enforce that measure, British troops were concentrated in Boston under General Gage. The colonists took counter-measures. The first Colonial Congress met in Philadelphia in September of 1774, at which twelve colonies were represented: Massachusetts, Connecticut, New Hampshire, Rhode Island, New York, New Jersey, Pennsylvania, Delaware, Maryland, Virginia, North Carolina, and South Carolina. Georgia was not present.

True to the best of English traditions, the Congress documented its attitude by a "Declaration of Rights." This Congress was practically an Insurrectionary Government, but no blow was struck until the Spring of 1775. Then came the first shedding of blood since March 5, 1770; the day of the Boston Massacre where American patriot Crispus Attacks (1723-1770) died for the right of the United States to exist as an independent nation. He was the first person killed in the massacre. Yes, a black man was the first to die for the love, dream, destiny, and greatness of the United Colonies of America. Two of the American leaders, John Hancock and Samuel Adams, had been marked and charged by the British government for arrest and trial for treason. They were known to be in Lexington, about eleven miles from Boston; and in the night of April 8, 1775, General Gage set his forces in motion for their arrests.

That night was a momentous one in history. The movement of Gage's troops had been observed; signal lanterns were shown from a Church tower in Boston, and two men, William Dawes and Paul Revere, stole away in boats across the back bay and took horses and warned the countryside. The British were ferried over the water, and as they marched through the night towards Lexington, the firing of single cannons and the ringing of Church bells went before them. As they entered Lexington at dawn, they were met by a small troop of men drawn up in military fashion. The British fired first; there was a shot and the exchanging of fire and with the British having more fire power, leaving eight dead and nine wounded upon the Village Green. The British then marched on to Concord, ten miles further, occupied the village, and stationed troops on the bridge there. The expedition and mission had failed in it's purpose of arresting Hancock and Adams, and the British commander was at a loss as to what to do next. Meanwhile the colonial drafts called "levies" in that time; were coming up from all directions. They bum rushed the British soldiers and forced them to retreat to Boston. However, while in the retreat, they were shot at and many picked off by drafts hiding behind rocks, fences and buildings. This is in addition to the heat of late New England spring. The British had reinforcements in Lexington where they briefly rested, then resumed their retreat to Boston and colonial drafts took their quarters in Cambridge and prepared to blockade the city.

So, "It was on." The war began. It was not only a war that promised a conclusive end. The United Colonies had no vulnerable Capital City or "Headquarters", if you will. They were dispersed over a great country with a limitless wilderness behind it; therefore they had great capabilities in terms of resistance. The colonists learned their tactics and strategies from the Indians. They could fight well in open field, and could rush and attack and kill troops in movement. Unfortunately, they had no disciplined Army that could beat nor equal the British in a pitched outright battle, they had very little military equipment; and their levies (drafts) grew impatient at a long tough campaign, and tended to go home to their farms. The British, on the other hand, had a well drilled Army, and their command of the sea gave them the power of shifting their attack up and down the long Atlantic seaboard. The British was at peace with all the world. But the King was greedy and stupid to interfere with such conduct in this state of affairs. He was in perfect position; worldwide, however greedy and stupid. The Generals he favored and selected were stupid; yet strong men but they were somewhat flighty men of reputation and fashion who were concerned with just that, not to complete the mission of England of conquest; which was the business at hand. The King chose the strategy of blockade, raid, and annoy the powerless colonists into submission and then a conclusive conquest and thus occupation of the land. Occupation of the land is important to long-term ownership and power. Throughout all of history occupation of land or right to ownership or the allowing of occupation or residency, under the rule of another.

But the methods employed by the British, and particularly the use of hired German troops, whom still retained the cruel traditions of the Thirty Years' War, and of Indian auxiliaries; were not good moves. The Congress, meeting for the second time in 1775, endorsed the actions of the New England colonists, and appointed George Washington as American Commander in Chief. The answer to this conflict was independence. It is interesting that at the outset of the war the colonists in general appeared to have been as little disposed to repudiate monarchy and claim complete independence as the Hollanders in the opening phase of Phillip II's persecutions and oppressions. The Separatists were called radicals; however, they were mostly extremely Democratic in today's terms, and their advanced views and ideals frightened many of the wealthier and established colonists, for whom class privileges and distinctions had considerable charm and advantage. But in early 1776, an enlightened and persuasive Englishman, Thomas Paine; perhaps the true father of "Separate but Equal" and the father most certainly of the independence of the United States of America published a pamphlet in Philadelphia called "Common Sense", which had an enormous effect on public opinion. Its style was rhetorical by today's literary standards. In The Blood of the Slain, the weeping voice of nature cries, "Tis Time To Part." Its' effects were very great. It converted tens of thousands to the ideal and necessity of separation. As always (as exhibited today) the turnover of opinion; once it had began, was rapid.

In the summer of 1776, July 4, 1776 to be exact; Congress took the irrevocable step of declaring for separation. The "Declaration of Independence," another of those exemplary documents which has been the peculiar service of the English to produce for mankind, was drawn up by Thomas Jefferson. And after various amendments and modifications, it was made the fundamental document of the United States of America. However there were two noteworthy amendments to Jefferson's draft. He denounced Slavery in the slave trade fiercely, and blamed the home government for interfering with the colonial attempts to end the slave trade. This was thrown out of the Declaration of Independence, as well as a statement about the British: "We must endeavour to forget our former love for the Crown; we might have been a free and great people together." At that point and within that time frame of days to construct a new nation, the United States of America had a real chance at perfection. Add the recognition and integration of the American Indians with the aforementioned deletions and we would have been building the United States of America in a completely righteous manner.

In 1777 British General John "Gentleman Johnny" Burgoyne, in an attempt into an attack and capture New York coming through Canada, was defeated at Freeman's Farm on the Upper Hudson, and surrounded and he was obliged to surrender at Saratoga with his entire army on July 6, 1777. This disaster encouraged the French and Spanish to come into the struggle on the side of the Colonists. The French Fleet did much to minimize the advantage of the British at sea. General Charles Cornwallis, 1st Marquis and 2nd Earl was caught in the Yorktown Peninsula in Virginia in 1781, and surrendered with his army. The British government, now heavily engaged with France and Spain in Europe, was at the end of its resources.

Towards the end of 1782 the preliminary articles of the treaty in which Britain

BIRTH OF A NATION

recognized the complete independence of the United States were signed in Paris. The end of the war was proclaimed on April 19, 1783, exactly eight years after Dawes and Revere's ride and the retreat of General Gages men from Concord to Boston. The Treaty of Peace was finally signed in Paris in September 1783. With the establishment of their independence came a new sort of community into the world. It was like something out of an egg. It was a Western European civilization that had broken free from the last traces of Empire and Christendom; and it had not a vestige of Monarchy left and no State Religion. It had no Dukes, Princess, Counts, nor any sort of title bearers claiming to ascendancy or respect as a right. Even its unity; however noble and of God (if they realized this or not), was yet a mere unity for defiance, defense, and freedom.

I submit to you that in the context of human history that it was in these respects such a clean start in political organization as the world had not seen before. The absence of any binding religious tie is especially noteworthy. It had a number of forms or rather, interpretations of Christianity, however its spirit was indubitably Christian; but as a State document of 1796 explicitly declared, the Government of the United States is not in any sense founded on the Christian Religion. This new community had, in fact, gone right down to the bare and stripped the fundamentals of human association, and it was building up a new sort of society and a new sort of state upon these foundations. Here we have about 4 million people scattered over a vast area with very slow and difficult means of intercommunication, poor as yet, but with potential of limitless wealth, setting out to do in reality on a huge scale such a feat of construction as the Athenian Philosophers twenty-two centuries before had done in imagination and theory.

This situation marks a definite step in the release of Man and from precedent in usage, and a definite step towards the conscious and deliberate reconstruction of his circumstances to suit his needs and aims. It was a new method being practical in human affairs. The modern state of Europe had evolved, institution by institution, slowly and painlessly out of preceding things. The United States of America was planned and made. In one respect, however, the creative freedom of the new nation was very seriously restricted. This sort of community and state was not built on a cleared site. It was not even an artificiality, as some of the Athenian Colonies which went out from the mother city to plan and build brand new city states with the brand new constitutions. By the end of the war, the Thirteen Colonies all had constitutions of their own. Either like that of Connecticut and Rhode Island, dating from their original charters (1662) or, as in the case of the rest of the States, where a British Governor had played a large part in the administration, re-made during the conflict. But we may as well consider these reconstructions as contributory essays and experiments in political and government sculpturing in the general constructive effort.

Upon the effort certain ideas stood very prominently. One was the idea of political and social equality. This idea, which came into the world as an extreme and almost incredible idea in the age between Buddha and Jesus Christ, is now asserted in the later 18th century as a practical standard of human relationships. So says the fundamental document of Virginia; "All men are by nature equally free and independent," and proceeds to rehearse their "rights," and to assert that all magistrates and Governors are but "Trustees and Servants," of the Commonwealth. All men are equally entitled to the free exercise of religion. The King; by right, the aristocrat, the natural slave, the God King, and God in all but vanished from this political scheme; so as far as declarations go. Most of the States produced similar preludes of the government. The Declaration of Independence said that all men are born equal. It is asserted everywhere in 18th century terms that the new community is to be; to use the terminology introduced early in the text; a Community of Will and not a Community Obedience. But the thinkers of the time had a rather clumsier way of putting the things they imagined a sort of individual choice of assent to citizenship than never in fact occurred; the so-called social contract. The Massachusetts Preamble, for instance, asserts that the State is a "Voluntary Association," by which the whole people covenants with each citizen and each citizen with the whole people that all shall be governed by laws for the common good.

Now, it will be evident that most of these fundamental statements are very questionable statements. The integrity of the documents were very questionable. In the reality of the time and period and the activities occurring therein; all men were not born equal, they were not all born free; they were born among a various multitude of men and women interwoven in an ancient, scripture, God-powered, difficult to interpret yet ecstasy which lies in its understanding; complex social net. Nor are all men invited to sign the social contract, or, failing that, to depart into solitude. These statements and documents were literally interpreted. They made them in order to express certain elusive but profoundly important ideas. Ideas that, after another century and a half of thinking, the world is in a better position to express. Civilization, as I have endeavored to point out, arose as a Community of Obedience, and was essentially a Community of Obedience. But generation after generation, even to this day in 2005 A.D. where I engage intellect and understanding; the spirit was abused by Priests. War is occurring in our present times is the manifestation of it long-term or should I say; of the historical problem of abuse of power and trust. Abuse of the faith of those among the Community of

BIRTH OF A NATION

Obedience; transferring and a Priest to Church D after questionable behavior at Church A, B, and C. As to date the spirit and the power continues to be abused by Priests and rulers.

There was a continual influx of masterful will from the forests, park lands and steppes. The human spirit had at last rebelled altogether against the blind obediences of the common life. It was seeking; and initially very clumsily seeking to achieve a new and better sort of civilization that should also be a Community of Will. To that end was necessary that every man should be treated as sovereign of himself; his standing was to be of Fellowship and not of Servitude. His real use, his real importance, depended upon his individual quality. Sounds familiar; the concepts and arguments of Martin Luther King, Jr. were rooted in individual quality and content of character therein. The methods which these creators of political America sought to secure this Community of Will was an extremely simple and crude one. They gave what was for the time mind you, and in consideration of American conditions, a very wide franchise. Conditions varied State by State. The widest and largest franchise was in Pennsylvania, where every adult male taxpayer voted; but, compared with Britain, all of the United States were well within sight of manhood suffrage by the end of the 18th century. These makers of America also made efforts; actually considerable for that time; but puny by more modern standards, to secure a widely diffused common education. The information to the citizens as to what was going on at home aboard, that they left, apparently without any arguments of wrong doing; to public meetings, and to the privately-owned printing press.

The story of the various State Constitutions and of the Constitution of the United States as a whole, is a very intricate one, and I do not have time to expound on all the details as much as I would like to; I must dig the hollow ground, the souls their need rest most. I have pointed out that slavery and the treatment of Indian Americans as permanent black eyes on the United States of America; however, another and to many, the most noteworthy point in a modern view, is the disregard of women and citizens. The American community was a simple, largely agricultural community, and most women were married; it seemed natural that they should be represented by their men folk. But New Jersey admitted a few women to vote on a property qualification basis. Another, yet an important point of interest then but continues to endure today is the point that it is almost of universal decision to have two governing assemblies, confirming or checking each other, founded on the model of the Lords and Commons of Britain. Only Pennsylvania had a single representative chamber, and that was felt to be very dangerous and Ultra - Democratic state of affairs. Apart from the argument that legislation should be slow as well as sure, it is difficult to establish any new necessity for this "Bicameral" arrangement. It appears to have been in fashion with Constitutional planners in the 18th century rather than a reasonable imperative. The British division was an old one: the Lords, the original Parliament, which was an assembly of "notables", the leading men of the kingdom; the House of Commons, which came in as a new factor as the elected spokesman of the complacent members of the middle class and the small land owning men.

It wasn't little too hastily assumed in the 18th century that the commonwealth would be given to wild impulses that would need checking; the opinion was for democracy, but for democracy with powerful brakes always on, whether if it was going uphill or down. In about all of the upper Houses there was, therefore, a flavor of selectiveness; they were selected and elected on a more limited franchise. This idea of making an upper chamber which shall be a stronghold for the substantial man did not appeal to modern thinkers so strongly as it gave to the men of 18th Century, but the bicameral idea is still alive, active and still has its importance. They suggested that a community may; with advantage, consider its affairs from two points of view---through the eyes of a body elected to represent trades, industries, professions, public services, and the like; a body representing function, and through the eyes of a second body elected by localities to represent communities. For the members of the former a man would vote by his personal, physical presence; for the latter by his district of residence. They point out that the British House of Lords is in fact a body representing function, in which the Land, the Law, and the Church are in no doubt disproportionately represented, but and which Industrialism, Finance, the Public Services, Art, Science, and Medicine also find places; and that the British House of Commons is purely geographical in this reference. It has been suggested in Britain that there should be "labor peers," selected from among the leaders of the great industrial trade unions.

The central government of the United States was initially a very feeble body, a Congress of Representatives of the Thirteen colonies; held together by the Articles of Confederation. The Congress was merely a conference of sovereign representatives; it had no control. For example, over the foreign trade of each state, it could not coin money nor levy taxes by its own authority. When John Adams, the first Diplomat/Prime Minister from the United States to England, went to discuss a Commercial Treaty with the British Foreign Secretary, he was met by requests for Thirteen Representatives, one from each State concerned. He had to confess inadequacy to make binding arrangements. The British then began dealing with each State separately over the head of the Congress, and they had retained possession of a number of post in the American territory around the Great

BIRTH OF A NATION

Lakes because of the inability of Congress to hold these regions effectively. In another urgent matter Congress proved equally feeble. To the west of the thirteen States stretched limitless lands to which settlers were now in ever increasing numbers. Each of the State's had undefinable claims to expansion Westward. It was evident to any clear sighted man that the jostling of these claims must lead in the long run to war. Finally a Constitutional Convention was called in 1787 in Philadelphia, and it was there that the present Constitution of the United States was on its broad lines hammered out. A great change of spirit had gone on during the intervening years, a widespread realization of the need for unity..

When the Articles of Confederation were drawn, men had thought of the people of Virginia, the people of Massachusetts, the people of Rhode Island, and the like; now appears a new conception, "The People of the United States." The new government, with the Executive President, the Senators, Congressmen, and the Supreme Court, that was now created, was declared to be "The Government of the People of the United States;" it was a synthesis and not a mere assembly. It said "We the People," and not "We the States," as Lee of Virginia bitterly complained. It was to be a "Federal" and not a Confederate Government. State by State the new Constitution was ratified, and in the Spring of 1788 the first Congress upon the new lines assembled in New York, and the Presidency of George Washington, who had been the national Commander-in-Chief throughout the War of Independence. The Constitution then underwent considerable revision, and Washington, DC upon the Potomac was built as the Federal Capital.

A black man named Benjamin Banneker (1731--1806) was one of the major architects and brain trust in the design and building of this Federal Province. I mentioned earlier in this chapter the Roman Republic, it's interesting mixture of modern features with dark superstition and primordial savagery, as the Neanderthal anticipation of the modern Democratic state. A time may come when people will regard the contrivances and machinery of the American Constitution as the political equivalents of the implements and contrivances of Neolithic Man; they had served their purpose as well, and under their protection the State had grown into one of the greatest, most powerful and most civilized communities that the world had ever seen. But there was no reason in that for regarding the American Constitution as a thing more final and inalterable than the elevated railways that once overshadowed many New York thoroughfares, or the excellent and homely type of house architecture that still prevails in Philadelphia. These things also have served a purpose, they have their faults, and they can be improved. Our political contrivances, just as much as our domestic and mechanical contrivances need to undergo constant revision as knowledge and understanding are obtained and grow.

Since the American Constitution was planned, our conception of history and our knowledge of collective psychology have undergone very considerable development. We begin to see many things in the problem of government to which the men of the 18th Century were blind; and courageous as their constructive disposition was in relation to whatever political creation that went before them, it fell far short of the boldness which we in these days realize to be needed if this great human problem of establishing a civilized Community of Will on Earth is to be solved. They took things for granted which we know now need to be made the subject of the most specific scientific, social study and the most careful adjustment. They thought it was only necessary to set up schools and colleges, with a grant of land for maintenance, and that they might then be left to themselves. However, education is not a weed which will grow lustily in any soil, it is a vital and delicate crop that may easily wilt and degenerate. We have learned today that the under development of Universities and educational machinery is like seeing under development of the brain and nerves, which hampers the growth of the social body.

By European standards, and by the standards of any State that has existed hitherto, the level of the common education of America was high; but by the standards of what it might be and what should be, America was as an uneducated country. Further, the fathers of America thought also that they had but to leave the press free, and everyone would live in the light. They did not realize that a free press could develop a sort of Constitutional venality because of its relationships with advertisers, and that large newspaper proprietors could become buccaneers of opinion and inspire wreckers of good beginnings. And, finally, the makers of America had no knowledge of the complexities of vote manipulation.

The science of elections was beyond their folk, they knew nothing of the need of the transferable vote to prevent the "Working" of elections by specialized organizations, and the crude and rigid methods they adopted left their political soul. Politics became a trade, and a very basic trade; decent and able men, after the first great period, drifted out of politics and into "business," and the strength of the State declined. Private Enterprise ruled in many matters of common concern, because political corruption made collective enterprise impossible. Yet the defects of the great political system created by the Americans of the Revolutionary period did not appear immediately. For the next century; the history of the United States was one of rapid expansion and energetic work unparalleled in the world's history. At the same time, the century was one of oppression, exploitation, and inhumanity.

BIRTH OF A NATION

And it is this which would manifest the Black-Eye on America.

* * *

CHAPTER III

THE GOOSE THAT LAID THE GOLDEN EGG

It is true that the founders were limited in knowledge and outlook; they were limited by the limitations of the time. Like many of today, they were men of mixed motives; good intentions and impulses arose in their minds, great ideas swept through them, but they could also be jealous, lazy, obstinate, greedy, vicious and pagan. If one were to write a true, full, and specific history of the making of the United States of America, it would have to be written with charity of high spirits as a splendid comedy rising to the pursuit of noble ends. And in no other period do we find the rich, tortuous inhumanity of the American story so finely displayed as in regard to the issue of Slavery. Slavery, having reference to the general question and problem of labor, was the test of this new soul in the world's history, the American soul.

Slavery began very early in the European history of America, and no European people who came to America can be found completely innocent in the matter. At a time when Germany was the moral whipping-boy of Europe, it is well to note that the German record is in this respect and manifestation, is best of all. Among the initial outspoken utterances against Negro slavery came from German settlers in Pennsylvania. However, the German settler was working with free labor upon a temperate countryside well North of the plantation zone; he was not under serious temptation in this matter.

American Slavery began with the enslavement of Native American Indians for gang work in mines and on plantations, and it is most interesting that I must mention in this literary endeavour that it was a wise man indeed, Las Casas (Bartolome' de Las Casa, "Apostle of the Indies" 1474-1566), the Spanish missionary who sought to abolish the oppression and enslavement of the Native people of the America's, who urged that Negroes should be brought to America to relieve his tormented Indian's protege'. The need for labor upon the plantations of the West Indies and the South was imperative. When the supply of Indian captives proved inadequate, the planters turned to the Negro; whose work and strength was far more than adequate. They also turned to the jails and poorhouses of Europe, for a supply of toilers.

Daniel Defoe's Moll Flanders elaborates on how the business of Virginian white slavery looked to an intelligent Englishman in the early 18th century. But the Negro came very early. The year of 1620 was the year that saw the Pilgrim fathers landing at Plymouth in New England; it had been an American institution for over a century and a half before the War of Independence. It was to struggle on for the better part of a century more. And today, even now, unfortunately but potentially forever, the moral struggle and "Black-Eye" on America continues. But the conscious of thoughtful men in the colonies was never quite cast upon this story, and it was one of the statements of Thomas Jefferson against the Crown and Lords of Great Britain that every attempt to ameliorate, end or, at least restrain the slave trade on the part of the Colonists had been checked and/or overruled by the great proprietary interest of the mother-country. In 1776 Lord Dartmouth wrote that the Colonists could not be allowed to "check or discourage a traffic so beneficial to the Nation."

With the moral and intellectual ferment of the revolution, the question of Negro slavery came right into the forefront of the public conscious. The contrast and the challenge glared upon the mind. "All men are by nature Free and Equal," as stated in the Virginia Bill of Rights. However outside in the sunshine, under the whip of the overseer, toiled the Negro slave. It bears great witness to the great change to human ideas since the Roman Imperial system dissolved under the Barbarian inrush, that there could be this heart searching. The conditions of industry, production, and land tenure had long prevented any recrudescence of gang slavery; but now the cycle had come full circle, and there were enormous immediate advantages to be reaped in mines, upon plantations, and upon great public works. It was revived; but against great opposition. From the outset of the revival there were protests, and they grew. The revival was also counter to the new conscious of mankind.

THE GOOSE THAT LAID THE GOLDEN EGG

History tells us that in many respects the gang slavery of the African, the "*Negro*," was worse than anything in the ancient world. Specifically horrible was the provocation by the trade of slave wars and manhunts in Western Africa, and the cruelties of the long Transatlantic voyage. These "poor creatures," as described in many literary expositions worldwide to date; I'll use the actual; the great-great grandfathers of the great-great grandfathers of African Americans to date; were packed on the ships with insufficient provisions of food and water, without proper sanitation, and without medicines. Many who could tolerate Slavery upon the plantations found the slave trade too much for their moral digestion. Three European nations were chiefly concerned in this dark business; Britain, Spain, and Portugal, because they were the chief owners of the new lands in America. The comparative innocence of the other European powers is to be ascribed largely to their lesser temptations. They were similar communities; in parallel circumstances they would have behaved similarly.

Throughout the middle of the 18th century there was an active agitation against Negro Slavery in Great Britain as well as in the States. It was estimated that in 1770 the issue came to a conclusive test in Britain before Lord Mansfield. A Negro named James Somersett had been brought to England from Virginia by his owner. James ran away, was captured, and violently taken on a ship to be returned to Virginia. However, he was extracted from ship by a "*Writ of Habeas Corpus*," the Latin term *habeas* [to have] and *corpus* [body]; a term utilized and recognized today. Lord Mansfield declared that Slavery was a condition unknown to English law, an "odious" condition; and Somersett walked out of the court a free man. The Massachusetts Constitution of 1780 had declared that "All men are born free and equal." A particular Negro, Quaco, put the Constitution to the test in 1783. In that year; at that point and time, the soil of Massachusetts became like the soil of Britain, intolerant of Slavery and the slave trade; to tread upon Slavery was to become truly free. At that time no other State in the United States followed this example. In the census of 1790, Massachusetts, separate of all the other States, "Returned No Slaves."

The State of Virginia and its position on the issue of Slavery was quite Interesting, because it reveals the peculiar difficulties and the "black-eye" of the Southern States. The great Virginian Statesmen George Washington and Thomas Jefferson condemned the institution of slavery, yet owned and utilized several slaves; they expressed that is was only because there was no other form of domestic service. Virginia had developed a strong party in favor of emancipating slaves; but they demanded that the emancipated slaves should leave the State within one year or be outlawed. They were alarmed at the possibility that a free barbaric Negro

Community, many of its members African-born and reeking with said traditions of cannibalism and secret and scary religious rituals, should arise beside them upon Virginian soil. Thus, when we consider that point of view; although morally and historically wrong, we could endeavour to see why it was that a large number of Virginians should be disposed to retain the mass of Negroes in the country under control as slaves, while at the same time they were bitterly opposed to the slave trade and the importation of any fresh blood from Africa. The free Negroes, one thought, might easily become a nuisance; indeed the free State of Massachusetts shortly thereafter closed its borders of entry.

The question of slavery; in an anthropological analysis, is overwhelmingly interesting. In the ancient world it was usually no more than a query of status between individuals who are racially identical. Merged in the United States with a different and yet deeply more profound query of relationship between the two races at opposite extremes of the human species [in their minds] and of the most contrasted types and culture; it is a question of morality. If the black man would have been white, there would be little to no doubt that slavery and the slave trade would have been written off, out, vanished from the United States within a short period following the Declaration of Independence as a natural consequence and amend the statements in the Declaration. Especially with the statements originally submitted by the originator of the historical and quite possibly the greatest document ever written; Thomas Jefferson. This document defined political and individual freedom and responsibility and the relationship of man seeking a new peace; the first ever written. I am compelled as an intellectual to acknowledge the attempt of Thomas Jefferson to end slavery and his writing of the Declaration of Independence and in the brilliance of the document in terms of evaluating the relationship of man, in terms of right and wrong, and in terms of establishing a precedent on governing men. The attempt to establish a Community of Will. As stated by a great man, "Evil flourishes when good men do nothing."

So slavery continued into yet another century. The 19th century where therein the inevitable and due conflict would arise. The first half of the 19th century, which had been an age of reaction and recovery in Europe; in America it was a period of exponential growth. The new method of transportation, the Steamboat and the Railway, as well as communications by way of the Electric Telegraph, came just in time to facilitate the movement of the population across the vast continent. Mountainous barriers separated not only communities but Rulers; the Roman Empire was an empire of high road and wheel, and its divisions and separations and collapse were due to the impossibility of maintaining swift communications city by city. The Western Europe that emerged from the Napoleon Era storm was divided into National States that were perhaps as large as they could become without loss of solidarity with highroad horse traction as their linking method. If the people [the free people] of the United States would spread over the American continent with only horse traction, rough terrain, and letter writing to keep them together, it was inevitable that differences in local economic conditions would have developed into different social types, that wide separation would have fostered differences in dialect and effaced sympathy, that the inconvenience of attending Congress in Washington would have increased with every advance of the frontier westward, until eventually the States would have fallen apart into a loose league of practically independent and divergent nations.

Wars for mineral wealth, for access to the sea, and so forth would have followed and America would have become another Europe. But the river steamboat, the railway, and the telegraph arrived in time to prevent the separation, and the United States became the first of a new type of modern transport nation, altogether larger, more powerful, and more conscious of its unity and the necessity of maintaining it; than any nation the world had ever seen before. For the tendency now in America was not to diverge but assimilate, and citizens from various parts of the State's grew not more but less unlike each other in speech and thought and habit. The United States was really not comparable to a European power such as France or Italy. It was a new and larger type of political organization. Empires had existed prior to this one in the world comparable in land mass and population to that of the States, however, they were basically accumulations of diverse tribute paying and adhering folk united only by a government. The unity of the United States was inherent. It was a community of convenience and outlook of 100 million men. The railways which intensified the conflicts and congestion of Europe and inventions which gave Europe greater destructive power, confirmed the free unity of the Republic of America. To Europe the innovation of steam power brought congestion; to America, opportunity. Yet the quest to present greatness and security, the population of America endured a phase of dire conflict. The river steamboat, the railways, the telegraph, and their accompanying facilities, did not come soon enough to affirm the deepening conflict of interest and ideas between the Southern slave-holding States and the free industrial North. The railways and steamboats at first gave intensity to the sharp conflict in an already established difference. There was a profound difference in spirit between the two sections of the United States, and the increasing unification due to the new means of transportation made the query whether the Southern or the Northern spirit should prevail an ever more urgent one.

There was little possibility of compromise. The Northern spirit was free and individualistic; the Southern spirit made for great estates and a conscious gentility ruling over an unrespected, oppressed, dusty subject multitude. The sympathies of British liberalism and radicalism were for the North, the sympathies of the British landlords and the British ruling class were for the South. Slave revolts were rare, but brought to life by The Honorable Nat Turner, Reverend, abolitionist; born in 1800; the first Black American Revolutionary, and interest to this conflict. Every territory was organized into a State, every new transportation into a fast-growing American system, became a field of conflict between the two ideas; whether it should become a State of free citizens or whether the estate system should prevail. The issue crept slowly to predominance in American affairs after the establishment of Missouri in 1821 and the establishment of Arkansas in 1836 as slave-holding States. From 1833 an American anti-slavery society was not merely resisting the extension of the institution, but agitating the whole country for its complete abolition. The issue was flamed into conflict over the admission of Texas to the Union. Texas had originally been a part of the Republic of Mexico, but it was largely colonized by Americans from the slave-holding States, and it seceded from Mexico and established its independence in 1836. A vigorous agitation for the annexation of Texas followed, and Texas was annexed in 1844 and admitted as a State in December 1845. Under Mexican Law slavery had been forbidden in Texas; but now the South claimed Texas for slavery; and got it. Further, a War with Mexico arising out of the Texas annexation added New Mexico and other areas to the United States, and those regions also permitted slavery.

The passing of a Fugitive Slave Bill increased the ability of white men to the use of many methods of catching and returning run-away slaves who had fled to free States. But, meanwhile, the development of ocean navigation was bringing in a swarm of immigrants from Europe to swell the spreading population of the Northern States, and raising Iowa, Wisconsin, Minnesota, and Oregon to State level gave the anti-slavery North the possibility of predominance both in the Senate and the House of Representatives. The cotton-growing South, irritated by the increasing threat of the Abolitionist Movement, and fearing the predominance in Congress, began to talk of succession from the Union. Southerners began to dream of annexations to the South of them in Mexico and the West Indies, and of a great Slave State, detached from the North and reaching from the Mason-Dixon Line to Panama. They were further helped by a racist Supreme Court with racist activist Chief Justice Roger Taney in the historically significant 1857 Supreme Court case of *Dred Scott vs. Sanford,* in which United States Supreme Court rule that the United States territories could not prohibit Slavery and that neither Free nor enslaved Negroes had constitutional rights.

THE GOOSE THAT LAID THE GOLDEN EGG

Dred Scott was born a slave in Virginia in 1795. His original name was Sam Blow. Peter Blow, his owner, moved him first to Alabama in 1818, then to St. Louis in 1830. After Blow died, his son sold Sam to John Emerson, a surgeon in the U.S. Army. In 1834 Emerson was transferred to Fort Armstrong, Illinois, where slavery was prohibited by the Northwest Ordinance of 1787.. The ordinance had allowed the then territories in the West to become States with the condition that they forbid slavery. Like many other slave owning army officers, Emerson did not believe that his posting in free states subjected him to Anti-slavery Laws, so he brought Sam with him. Two years later Emerson was transferred to Fort Snelling; what is now Minnesota but was then part of the Wisconsin Territory. Slavery in the territory was banned by the Missouri Compromise of 1820, in which Congress decided that with the exception of Missouri, Slavery would be prohibited in the territories North of latitude to 36° to 30'.

At Fort Snelling, Sam married Harriet, the slave of another Army officer, and in 1838 the couple returned with Emerson to St. Louis. At some point in these moves, Sam took the name Dred Scott, which may have been a joke contrasting his tiny stature with that of the corpulent General Winfield "Great" Scott. In 1834 Emerson died and left his property, including Slaves, in trust to his wife. In 1846, with the help of his friends, Scott sued Mrs. Emerson in local court for his family's freedom. His lawyers argued that the Scotts' stay in free territory had Emancipated them, citing several precedents in Missouri case law, most important of which was *Racheal vs. Walker* (1837). The Scotts lost the case, moved for the verdict to be set aside, and in a new trial in 1850 won their freedom. Mrs. Emerson appealed to the Missouri Supreme Court which issued in a 2-to-1 decision in 1852, returned the Scotts to slavery. The court stated earlier court precedents, including its own, were made under circumstances that were no longer valid. Noting the rise of abolitionism In the country, the court argued that the of anti-slavery movements threatened to the "overthrow and destruction of our government." Thus Slave States should not be expected to uphold the law of Free States, and a Slave, whether on free soil or not, was still a Slave. This case was a forceful rejection of the Missouri Compromise. Mrs. Emerson's brother, John Sanford of New York, shortly thereafter, took over the affairs of her estate. In 1853 Scott filed suit against Sanford, this time in Federal Court. Scott argued that because he and Sanford lived in different states, the case required a federal trial. Sanford argued that Scott was still a slave and even if he were free, a black descendents of slaves were not entitled to bring suit. The Federal Court in St. Louis rejected Sanford's argument that free blacks could not bring suit, but concluded that Scott was still a slave. Scott appealed, and in 1856 U.S. Supreme Court heard his case.

Not wanting to affect the Presidential elections of 1856, the court postponed its ruling in Scott vs. Sanford until two days after President James Buchanan's inauguration. On March 6, 1857, a mostly Southern 7-to-2 majority found that Scott was still a slave. The court therefore needed only to agree with the lower court, remand parts of the decision that needed clarification, and be done with the case. However, several recent events conspired to put pressure on the court to make additional rulings that would settle the question of slavery. Chief among these events was Congress's 1850 passage of the Fugitive Slave Act, which placed severe penalties on Northerners who helped runaway slaves. Northern states responded by enacting laws to obstruct Southerners trying to capture runaway slaves. In 1854 Congress passed the even more controversial Kansas - Nebraska Act. The act largely overturned the Missouri Compromise by letting territories choose or reject slavery instead of leaving that decision to the Federal Government. The territory's right to choose, known as *popular sovereignty*, prompted intense conflicts in the territories and earned Kansas the label Bleeding Kansas.

Against this backdrop, Chief Justice Roger B. Taney decided to use Scott vs. Sanford to address the constitutionality of slavery. Writing for the court, he gave an extremely narrow interpretation of the Constitution's view of blacks. Taney began by arguing that the Constitution did not allow Congress to regulate slavery; or anything else; in the territories. Rather, the Constitution's statements about regulating territories applied only to those territories in the United States possession in 1789, when the Constitution was ratified.   Since the United States acquired the Louisiana Territory through the Louisiana Purchase in 1803, Congress had no power to regulate Purchase territories until they became States. The ruling effectively made the Missouri Compromise unconstitutional; this was only the second time that the Supreme Court had declared a Statute of Congress unconstitutional, the first being *Marbury vs. Madison* in 1803. Chief Justice Taney's ruling on the Missouri Compromise was especially unnecessary since the Kansas - Nebraska Act superseded.

Taney also interpreted the Constitution's Fifth Amendment, which prohibits the taking of property without due process of law, to apply to slaves. He argued that since slaves were property, they cannot be taken from their owners, regardless of whether they had crossed into a free State or territory. He further asserted that the Constitution never intended Blacks; even free Blacks in free states; to be citizens. Therefore, even if Scott were free, he was not entitled to bring a suit in a federal court. Supreme Court Chief Justice Taney, in perhaps the best-known sentence of his opinion, characterized Blacks as *"beings of an inferior order and altogether unfit to associate with the white race, either in social or political relations; and so*

THE GOOSE THAT LAID THE GOLDEN EGG

far inferior, that they had no rights that the white man was bound to respect; and that the Negro might justly and lawfully be reduced to slavery for his benefit".

Justices Benjamin R. Curtis and John McLean dissented. They cited accounts showing that many Blacks were citizens both before and after the ratification of the Constitution, and they argued that the authors of the Constitution fully intended its protection to apply to them. Therefore, they said, Scott had the right to sue. They also argued that the Constitution intended Congress to regulate all United States territories at all times, not just territories controlled by the states in 1789. Finally, a law banning slavery freed any slave who entered the law's jurisdiction, Scott and his family were freed by virtue of their stay on free soil and could not be returned to slavery after returning to a slave state. Soon after the Supreme Court issued its decision, Dred Scott and his wife and two daughters were sold to a son of Peter Blow, the Scott's original owner, who freed them immediately. Unfortunately, Scott did not live long enough to see the many changes his case brought about. In September of 1858 Dred Scott died of tuberculosis in St. Louis. The ruling, one of the most infamous in the Supreme Court history stimulated controversy and made abolitionism, which had struggled for respectability, a more popular stance. Even Northerners who did not care about slavery in the territories worried that Scott vs. Sanford could be used to legalize Slavery in the North. Understand that the issue of Slavery could have easily separated the United States of America.

What is now the State of Kansas became the region and the stage for the final showdown. The Slavery Issue plunged the Territory of Kansas into what was practically a Civil War between the free settlers and the immigrants from the Slave States; a war that continued until 1857 and ended in the victory of the anti-slavery settlers. It took until 1861 before Kansas was raised to Statehood. The continuation of Slavery was the chief issue before the country in the Presidential election of 1860, and the appearance of Abraham Lincoln as an Anti-Slavery President inclined the South to leave and split the Union. South Carolina passed an "Ordinance of Secession," and prepared for war. Mississippi, Florida, Alabama, Georgia, Louisiana, and Texas joined her in early 1861, and a convention was assembled in Montgomery, Alabama. The assembly elected Jefferson Davis as President of "The Confederate States of America" and had the unmitigated gull to write and adopt a Constitution similar to that of the Constitution of the United States, yet specifically upholding "The Institution of Negro Slavery."

Such was the political situation which Abraham Lincoln was called to deal with as President of the Union. Lincoln was a man entirely typical of the new people that had grown up after the War of Independence. His family were quite common folk; by societal standards. His father could not read nor write until after he married Lincoln's mother; who was said to be an illegitimate child. She was quite sharp and of great character and belief. Lincoln is truly a paramount figure in the evolution and sustaining of the United States of America. Lincoln's early years had been spent as a drifting particle in the general westward flow of the population. He was born in Kentucky in 1809, was taken to Indiana as a boy, and later on to Illinois. His early education was poor and casual; however, his mother taught him to read early, and he became a voracious reader. At 19, he went down river to New Orleans as a hired hand on a flat boat. He worked for a time as a store clerk in a store, served as a volunteer in an Indian War, and went into business as a storekeeper with a drunken partner, and contracted debt that took him 15 years to pay off. When he was 24 he obtained a job as a Deputy to the County surveyor of Sangamon County, Illinois. All the while he was reading hard. He knew his Shakespeare and Burns well, the life of Washington, of Jefferson, and the history of the United States, and so forth. He had the instinct for expression, and from his boyhood he wrote as well as he studied; producing verse, essays, and the like.

Politics soon attracted Lincoln. In 1834, when he was only 25, he was elected Member of the House of Representatives for the State of Illinois. He read for the Bar; and was admitted in 1836. For a time he worked more in the practice of law than politics. However, the great query before the people of the United States demanded the attention of every able man. This tall, capable, self-educated man from the mid-west of America, would not fail to be profoundly stirred by the growing development of the issues of slavery and succession. In Illinois it was quite interesting because the respected Congressional leader of the party for the continuation of Slavery was Senator Stephen Douglas of Illinois. There was a personal rivalry between Lincoln and Douglas; they both dated the woman who became Mrs. Lincoln. Douglas was a man of ability and prestige, and for some years Lincoln fought against him verbally and by prose, first in Illinois and then throughout the Eastern States, rising steadily to the position of his most formidable and eventually victorious antagonist.

Their culminating struggle was the Presidential Campaign of 1860, and on March 4, 1861, Lincoln was inaugurated President of the United States, with the Southern States already in active succession and committing acts of war. The first proceeding of the successionist South was the seizure of all Federal forts and stores within their boundaries. These Federal Posts' were built on real estate belonging to the States' ; and these States claimed the right to "resume" their real estate. The Garrison of Fort Sumter in Charleston resisted, and the war began with the bombardment of this Fort on April 12, 1861. America at that time had

THE GOOSE THAT LAID THE GOLDEN EGG

only a very small regular army; it remained loyal to the President. The opening operations of the Confederacy were conducted by State levies. President Lincoln immediately called for 75,000 men; and Tennessee, Arkansas, North Carolina, and Virginia immediately went over to the Confederacy, which had the unmitigated gull to hoist its own flag, the "Stars and Bars" against America's "Star and Stripes."

Thus, began the United States of America's Civil War. A war which continued to define the evolving United States. A war which was in an overall sense; unnecessary. A war which could have been never thought of or endeavoured if the concepts and original writings of the Declaration of Independence by Thomas Jefferson were adhered to and not eliminated from the document by the other founding fathers. Finally, a war which resulted in the use of and death of thousands and thousands of men. The bad use of good men. It was fought by improvised armies that grew continuously from tens of thousands to hundreds of thousands; until at last the Federal forces of the Union exceeded 1,000,000 men. It was fought over a vast territory which spread from New Mexico to the Eastern/Atlantic seaboards. The ultimate objective of the Confederacy was to capture Washington D.C. The planned goal of the Union was to capture Richmond, Virginia.

The Confederates, outnumbered and far poorer in resources, were fortunate with regard to their military leadership. They fought under a General of great ability, General Lee. The Generals of the Union were not as good as General Lee. For some time President Lincoln clung to McClellan, the "young Napoleon," a pedantic, dilatory, and disappointing Commander. He dismissed and appointed many Generals including McClellan, Polk, Burnside, Hooker, and others who led and lost thousands of Union troops in Fredericksburg, Virginia and in Chancellorville where on April 30, 1863 General Hooker lost 17,000 men to Stonewall Jackson, giving General Lee his greatest victory (although Jackson lost 13,000 men) because Lee outsmarted Hooker by being prepared for his planned attack. The Generals of the Union consciously did not take advantage of opportunities to crush and/or capture the Confederates and potentially end the war. Such as after the great Battle of Gettysburg when Confederate General Pickett led his troops into a planned attack in which a total of 51,000 men died. General Lee and the Confederates, having lost 28,000 men in Pickett's charge on Gettysburg; were beaten men, retreating men. General Meade of the Union; did not attack. Lincoln was again outraged; he was tired of having to push and motivate and nearly force his Generals to attack and take advantage of situations.

Finally, Lincoln put in General U. S. Grant and General Sherman; whom delivered victory over the ragged and depleted South. But this four year struggle had meant enormous physical and moral strain for the people of United States.

America: Birth to Greatness and the Black Man's Contribution

In many States such as Maryland and Kentucky, public opinion upon the war was acutely divided. The principle of State autonomy was very important to many citizens, and the North seemed to many to be in effect to be forcing the abolition of slavery upon the South. Many men were against slavery, but also against the interference with "The Free People," and the "Free Power" of each individual State over its own people. The manifestation of domination. In England, it was predicted that the South would win the war. By the Summer of 1862, Lincoln knew that the answer was the emancipation of slaves. His primary theme was to preserve the Union.

Following the abolition of slavery; the wrong which must be made right. In the border States brothers and cousins, even fathers and sons, would take opposite sides and found themselves in antagonistic Armies. The North believed that its cause was a righteous one, but for many people it was not a full-bodied and unchallenged righteousness. But for Lincoln, there was no doubt. He was a clear minded man in the midst of such confusion. He stood for the Union; he stood for the great peace of a United America. He was opposed to slavery, but slavery he held to be a secondary issue. His primary goal was that America should not be torn into two contrasted, morally opposite, jarring fragments. Thus, through the long four years of struggle he stood with an inflexible conviction; a steadfast will.

Frederick Douglass, Black America's founding father, was writing vigorously in his publication, The North Star; about how paramount the issue of slavery was to America. Talking with President Lincoln on occasion; Frederick Douglass said that the very destiny of America's lies in our dealing with the Institution of Slavery. Frederick Douglass is a founding father of the recognition of the Negro intellect, investment, and belief in America as are Crispus Attacks and Benjamin Banneker, Nat Turner, Sojourner Truth, and Harriet Tubman are founding parents of Black America because of their ability and willingness to advocate and represent the sacrifice, the ability, and perseverance of the Negro. It is much to their work, struggle and sacrifice to just prepare a path, that is the carpet we walk on today; we owe. Lincoln stated on September 3, 1862 that if he could save the Union by freeing part of the slaves he would; if he could save the Union by freeing slaves and a certain region, he would; but the only way to save the Union was to free them all. To Emancipate them all. And on September 22, 1862 President Lincoln executed the Emancipation Proclamation. Our ancestors were officially free. And on December 31, 1862 at Boston Music Hall, William Lloyd Garrison, a great and honorable white abolitionist and leader who founded and published the Anti-Slavery Journal, cried next to Frederick Douglass and Harriet Tubman when the Proclamation was being read to the crowd. However, the Union remained in an

THE GOOSE THAT LAID THE GOLDEN EGG

internal war.

As the war dragged on through 1862 and 1863, the first passions and enthusiasms waned, and America obtained an education on the phases of war, it's weariness and it's disgust. Conscription replaced volunteering and changed the spirit of the fighting both in the South and the North. The war became a prolonged, dismal, fratricidal struggle. The first draft in the United States came from Jefferson Davis, President of the Confederate States of America. He ordered every white man from age 18 to 36 to report and join the Confederate Army. 40% of the eligible men signed up; the other 60% refused. Lincoln insisted on the draft in 1863, which had resistance as well. In July of 1863, New York endured rioting against the drafts. On July 14, 1863, Irish citizens rioted in New York, continuing for three days, killing several black people, burning Black Churches and looting. There was, however, a stipulation in the draft which allowed an individual to pay the sum of $300 to be waived from the draft. Andrew Carnegie, J.P. Morgan and other early big-money movers and shakers in American Industry paid not to go. The Democratic Party in the North sought to win the Presidential Election of 1864 on the plea that the war was a failure and should be ceased. This would, of course, had meant a practical victory for the South. There were planned and organized conspiracies to defeat the draft. The gaunt focused man in the White House found himself dam near surrounded by defeatist, traitors, sell-outs, dismissed Generals, torturous party politicians and a somewhat doubting and fatigued people behind him, and uninspired non-strategic minded General's and depressed soldiers before him. I understand and appreciate the stress filled look on his face which shines on the Five Dollar Bill of United States Currency. Further, I understand and appreciate his statement, "What we do today is not for today."

The Black man played an interesting and crucial role here. Frederick Douglass said that the Negro was the key figure in the war. The Union General Ulysses S. Grant said that by arming the Negro, he will make a great soldier. General Grant was correct, for the Black man was fighting for his right to be free and the right to choose to fight. 180,000 Civil War soldiers were Black men who fought bravely and victoriously, such as the Massachusetts 54th Regiment who on July 18, 1863 at Battery Wagner/Fort Wagner, achieved a key Union victory. At that moment, in the Summer of 1863 General Lee felt invincible because of decisive victories for the Confederacy such as in Chancellorville. The battle resulted in the loss of 17,000 Union troops led by General Joe Hooker. However the Confederate victory cost Stonewall Jackson 13,000 men of his own. Stonewall died shortly thereafter. But the decisive victories for the Union in the fall of 1863 such as the great defeat of Confederate General Pickett, whose men were slaughtered as the Union soldiers shouted "Fredericksburg," recalling the slaughter endured by the Union which was also due to poor military strategic planning.

The stage was set for one of, if not the greatest speech ever delivered, in terms of solidifying and expanding a nation and bringing into context the reality of the Civil War and healing the deep wounds endured within the process. The battle in Gettysburg cost America 51,000 lives and a major victory for the Union. At a specific cost of 23,000 Union soldiers, the Confederacy suffered a devastating loss of 28,000 soldiers. The war could have been potentially over then if General Meade, another incompetent Union General, would have attacked General Lee's retreating Army. General Lee's, at that point; beaten Army. This inability to siege war advantage, again outraged President Lincoln.

The speech to place at Union Cemetery in Gettysburg, Pennsylvania on November 19, 1863. Edward Everett, United States Secretary of State spoke for two hours on International interest and perspective; and President Lincoln delivered 269 words which addressed and answered questions and concepts of 1776, and perspective and simultaneously gave life to the overdue baby of a Nation. The Gettysburg Address attributed specific regard of the past; a true interpreting and acceptance of the present; and the challenging yet acknowledged goal of the future of a United States of America. As 1863 ended and 1864 began, the new year brought new changes, challenges, and brutality for the Black man; worldwide.

In 1864, the British drove of the Besoto Tribe out of Africa. In 1864, a barrel of flour cost $250, a stick of fire would cost $5.00. In 1864, the Ku Klux Klan was born. In 1864, the 13th Amendment, officially confirming President Lincoln's Emancipation of slaves was ratified in Congress. In 1864, General Lee asked the unreleased slaves to fight for the Confederacy, promising freedom and going further to state that the Yankees only wanted to use Negroes to pull their carriages. They were able to get a few. These are not to be considered sell-outs in any shape, form, or fashion; they were attempting to secure a better life for their children and their children's children. Now at the same time, the French Army was trampling the Monroe Doctrine in the dirt. Subtle proposals came from Jefferson Davis from Richmond; Confederate headquarters to drop the Civil War, leave the issues of the war to subsequent discussion and allow the Union and the Confederacy to act as allies to defeat the French in Mexico. However, Lincoln would not hear of such proposals unless the supremacy of the Union was maintained. He stated that Americans might do such things as one people, but not as two. He held the United States together through long weary months of back and forth, ineffective effort, through tough phases of divisions and failing and/or lack of courage; with no record of faltering or discouraged with his purpose. As stated earlier in the text; a steadfast will.

In the Presidential Election of 1864, the Democratic Party nominated General McClellan in an all out effort to defeat Lincoln, with the power players on both Democratic and Republican parties opposing him. The Presidential Election of 1864 became a referendum in itself. Lincoln defeated McClellan easily and became the second president to be re-elected since Andrew Jackson. The will of the people was with Lincoln. In the earlier months of 1865 with a Union victory close at hand, Lincoln met with all of his Generals in order to make the Confederate surrender as easy as possible and give the power and support to the beginning of reconciliation. As always Lincoln's key word was "Union," and he didn't want to badly embarrass the South. He entered Richmond the day after its surrender and personally received General Lee's capitulation.

He returned to Washington, and on April 11, 1865 made his last public address. His theme was reconciliation and the reconstruction of loyal government in the defeated States. Three days thereafter, on the evening of April 14, 1865, he went to Ford's Theater in Washington, and as he sat looking at the stage he was shot in the back of the head and cruelly assassinated by an actor named Booth, who crept into the Presidential Box unnoticed. John Wilkes Booth was a fervent and radical advocate of slavery, yet never had the heart to fight in the war. Booth described himself as a worthless coward and he is due no further discussion in this text. The task of healing and righting the wrongs was impaired and the bitterness and devilishness that developed after the war, only took place because Lincoln was dead. But his great task was done, and the Union was saved, and saved for good. He ended the institution of slavery, although not having time to implement his plan for compensation to slaves. His plan for compensation of 40 acres and a mule would not take place. It went unfulfilled because only Lincoln possessed the integrity and the spirit of righteousness to see it through. And to this very day, no President of the United States has had the integrity and spirit of righteousness to bare mere discussion on the subject.

Lincoln's endeavour warrants respect; more than any President of the United States thereafter; if not for Lincoln there would not be a United States of America. At the beginning of the war there was no railway to the Pacific Coast; now the railways spread like a rapidly growing plant until it intertwined and clutched and woven all the vast territories of the United States into one now unbreakable mental and material unity. From that time the consolidation of the United States proceeded steadfastly. This somewhat titanic democracy, without Kings and Queens or ruler or elaborate foreign policy, was, as stated previously, a new thing in the world's experience. However, this great and effective democracy, or at least evolving to greatness, effective and ongoing politically, was socially, totally unfair, unjust, and oppressive to the Negro. It is important to note that just prior to the Civil War there was conflict among our Negro forefathers over what would be the best course of action for them and their anticipated forthcoming freedom. Should they return to Africa or emigrate to Latin America? Why Latin America? We can never be certain of the total number of Africans who arrived in the Americas as slaves. Scholarly estimates today range from 10 to 12 million. Countless others died on the African coast awaiting shipment or perished during the Transatlantic passage. Of the survivors, about 95% went to the Caribbean and Latin America.

Portugal's Brazil received the largest share of Africa's children, nearly 5 million; the Spanish Colonies received about 5 million. Most of the remainder went to British, French, Dutch, and Danish Colonies in the Caribbean. About 500,000 slaves were delivered to the mainland North of Spanish Florida. Although the slave population of the United States numbered 4 million and 1860, most of these brothers and sisters were born in America. Spared some of the full impact of diseases that devastated slaves in the tropics, the North American slave population was able to stabilize and reproduce itself naturally from the early decades of the 18th century. This may provide the North American Negro with the desire for success and progress with an increased hunger because of being a part of North America's fabric and growth. Although equal access may not exist; however, the innovation, creativity and willingness to sacrifice for success is inherit and a constant.

The two aforementioned questions of returning to Africa or emigrate to Latin America indeed had merit, but the third option was one of great merit and demanded consideration. Its theme; to remain in the United States and fight and struggle for racial equality and fair treatment. These options gave birth to the first debate among Negro intellectuals who were credible and respected and with special vision in terms of the understanding and dealing with the North American experience. Some Negroes in America showed an interest in returning to Africa before the 1860's, in the face of the criticism of black abolitionists such as Frederick Douglass who considered the American Negro dream of Africa was a dream of dangerous diversification of energies which were needed in the fight for Emancipation and Civil Rights in America. Interestingly ironic, one of the major pre-Civil War Negro advocates of the "Back to Africa'" dream was Martin R. Delany. This Harvard trained physician and the first Negro to be commissioned with field rank by President Lincoln. He traveled to Liberia in July 1859, and saw in the

THE GOOSE THAT LAID THE GOLDEN EGG

proposed Liberian Colony as a grand step in the march of African regeneration and Negro nationality. It was also in 1859 that Delany originated and expressed the phrase "Africa for the Africans." However, many contemporary black nationalists believe that Marcus Garvey, the great nationalist leader of the 1920's invented the term.

Delany was the co-editor with Frederick Douglass of the leading abolitionist publication, The North Star, founded in 1847 and his presence advocated the nationalist element of the early Nationalist vs. Integration argument. The true challenge was to stay in the United States and fight and obtain true Emancipation and Civil Rights at home; America. Rights which should have been a done deal on the basis of sweat equity in its purest sense. Rights earned through sweat, oppression, and sacrifice with the birth, growth, and dominance of the United States of America. Sweat and toil to facilitate the growth were not the only methods of contribution to the greatness of America; the inventions and innovations which fortified the superiority in industry and in global power. It is here where we enter the nucleus of our text, the gift to America and the world; the Negro; the African. Although he has lost his way along God's path; the Negro has exhibited and still possesses gifts of progress to mankind.

* * *

CHAPTER IV

INVESTMENT IN AMERICA

The Negro bestowal to the world is illustrated primarily by presence, toil, and endurance. Followed by overcoming, invention and innovation; unquestionable contributions. I submit to you that this goes back further than one may think. The African Slave Trade was already over 100 years old when the Dutch ship landed 20 Africans at the Jamestown Colony in 1619. Portugal had introduced Africans to Europe in the early 16th century. The Slave Trade soon extended into England and Spain and to their Colonies in the new world of the Americas when they were discovered. Africans accompanied the explorers on their journeys to the new world. There were 30 Africans with Vasco Nunez de Balboa (1475-1517) when he discovered and claimed the Pacific Ocean for Spain in 1513. Africans accompanied Francisco Pizarro (1475-1541) when the Spanish explorer who was the first European to explore the American Southwest, and with Cabeza de Vaca (1490- 1557) when he and Narvaez explored what is today Florida, Texas, and Mexico. Africans accompanied the French explorers to Canada and the Mississippi River Valley. Thus, Negroes were a part of the New World long before the Mayflower, even before the settling of Jamestown in 1609; and the indentation and contribution and investment in the growth and greatness of America and the world is significant.

The successful design and development of our nation's capital, Washington, D.C. was thanks to the contribution and brilliance of a Negro. Benjamin Banneker was placed on the planning committee to develop the District of Columbia at the request of Thomas Jefferson. The wisdom of Jefferson's appointment was evident soon thereafter and continues to endure today. Pierre L'Enfant, the famed French architect of both talent and arrogance, was hired to lead the designing process of implementation. L'Enfant was fired because of his bad temper which accompanied his arrogance. He departed Washington taking all of the design plans with him. In two days, or in our current appreciation of time, in 48 hours Benjamin Banneker recreated the complete layout of the streets, the parks, and major buildings; all from memory and his innovation. This contribution saved the United States Government innumerable time, money, and work. The years prior to that, during the Revolutionary War, wheat grown on a farm designed by Banneker prevented United States soldiers from starving. He invented a system of irrigation that was so reliable that it enabled their crops to flourish even during dry spells. Known as the first Black inventor, Banneker; the son of two freed slaves, grew up on his family's farm in Maryland where he cultivated his curiosity and love of the way things work.

At the age of 21 he saw the watch of his friend, Josef Levi. Banneker was so overwhelmingly fascinated by the watch that Levi soon thereafter gave it to him. Banneker immediately took the watch apart, studying each and every component and mechanism. He carved watch parts and mechanisms out of wood and made the first striking clock to be completely made in America. This clock was famous worldwide for its accuracy, keeping perfect time for well over 50 years. After his parents died, Banneker spent his time teaching himself astronomy through the books he borrowed from his friends. He built a work cabin with a skylight (think of the innovation), to study the stars and spending hour upon hour looking up into the heavens. He soon began to predict Solar and Lunar eclipses. The compiled results were published in his almanac which became a best seller from Maryland to Kentucky. Without any formal training or education in Science, Engineering, Architecture, Agriculture, or Astronomy; this man formulated, created, and innovated. This brother tapped into his God-given ability and his purpose, followed it and pursued the answers to the questions of his time and beyond. We must remember to dwell not on what we do not have; but to strive for progress and success with the blessings and abilities we do have. It is important for us to convey to the youth that adequate tools are available today to do great things and that their great-great-great grandparents did great things with significantly less.

Let us look at some other contributions of great significance. In 1862, sugar processing and the production and trade relating thereto, was a big business due to huge demand for sugar. However, supplying this demand came with strenuous and costly work. A Black man by the name of Norbert Rillieux engaged in the research and invention of a device that revolutionized sugar processing. Born in New Orleans, Louisiana in 1806, Rillieux's mother had been a slave and his father was a wealthy white sugar plantation owner. His brilliance was noticed at an early age. He was educated in Paris, France, and later taught engineering in Paris. Rillieux also published several steam engineering articles and writings. While in Paris, Rillieux learned that the boiling point of liquid is reduced as the pressure is reduced; much like a vacuum, and applied this concept to the processing of sugar; heating the cane sugar in a vacuum, and re-using the steam in the processing procedure. Rillieux's Multiple Effect Vacuum Sugar Evaporator, patented in 1864, make the processing of sugar more efficient, faster, and much safer. This resulted in a highly efficient mechanical process that replaced the old, laborious, dangerous, and costly methods of processing sugar by hand which was called the "Jamaica Train." Further, in addition to these great benefits, the end product was far more superior to any ever produced. Rillieux's invention was eventually adopted by sugar processing plants around the world. So the next time you are enjoying your coffee or favorite desert, give thanks to Norbert Rillieux and his contribution; making sugar truly sweet.

In 1872 the factors of necessity, brilliance, and opportunity intersected and changed the efficiency in the operation of machinery forever. In 1872 Elijah McCoy produced his first invention which was a revolutionary way of lubricating steam engines without having to shut them down. This was quite significant; for the Automatic Lubricator saved an enormous amount of time, money, and work in transportation and in industrial production. McCoy, born in Colchester, Ontario, Canada in 1843, was the son of George and Emilia McCoy, two former slaves who fled from the United States. He was educated as a mechanical engineer in Edinburgh, Scotland and returned to the United States to Detroit, Michigan. However despite his impressive education and skills for any man, of any race, creed, or color; he was a Black man, and could only get a job as a Fireman and as an Oilman on a Steam Engine Train shoveling coal into the train's engine and periodically lubricated the engine. McCoy recognized the inefficiency of the process and proceeded to invent the Automatic Lubricator. An invention which immediately improved the process and immediately changed things. His inventions were numerous to say the least, with a total of 57 patents and McCoy was known throughout the world for his work. In fact, among McCoy's most popular inventions was the oil-dripping cup for trains. The oil-dripping cup was so effective and popular that other inventions tried to copy his design. However, none of the other cups worked as well as McCoy's, so customers started asking for "The Real McCoy". This where the expression "The Real McCoy" comes from.

Deeper into our theme, I ask you to consider; if you will, a man who was forced to leave school at age 10 would be able to successfully patent over 35 Electrical and Mechanical inventions. Furthermore, a Black man. Granville T. Woods did just that, educating himself outside of school in practical skills for his future. Born in Columbus, Ohio on April 23, 1856, Woods literally learned his skills on the job. Attending school in Columbus until age 10, he served as an apprentice in a machine shop and acquired the skills and trade of Blacksmith and Machinist. During his youth he also went to night school and took private lessons. Although he had to forsake his formal education at age 10, Granville realized that education was essential to developing critical skills. Education, which would facilitate his success. Skills enabling him to use the platform of America to express his brilliance and creativity.

In 1872 he acquired a job as a Fireman on the Danville & Southern Railroad in Missouri, eventually becoming an engineer. He invested his spare time in electronics. In 1874 Woods moved to Springfield, Illinois to work in a rolling mill. He relocated to the East in 1876 and worked part-time in a machine shop and took a mechanical engineering course at an Eastern College. In 1878 he became an engineer aboard the Ironsides, a British Steamer, and within two years, he became Chief Engineer of the steamer. Even with his impressive background and with all of his engineering skill, he was unable to progress in any of these jobs. His travels and experiences led him to settle in Cincinnati, Ohio. Granville was a great electrician and inventive genius whose talents could not go unrecognized.

By 1880, Granville had established his own shop in Cincinnati and brought in his brother Lyates to organize the Woods Electrical Company. A few years later, he successfully sold several of his inventions to the biggest and best corporations in the United States. He was able to sell many of his inventions to American Bell Telephone Company, General Electric, and Westinghouse Air Brake Company. In 1888 Woods developed and patented a system for overhead electric conducting lines for railroads, which aided in the development of the Overhead Railway System found in contemporary metropolitan cities such as Chicago, St. Louis, and New York City. In his early 30's, he became interested in thermal power and steam driven engines. And in 1889, he filed his first patent for an improved Steam Boiler Furnace. In 1892, his brilliance resulted in The Electric Railway System (U.S. Patent# 463,020) which was operated in Coney Island, New York, completely electric. The railway system had no exposed wires, secondary batteries, or slotted causeway --- all previously necessary for electric railways.

In 1887 he patented the Synchronous Multiplex Railway Telegraph (U.S.

INVESTMENT IN AMERICA

Patent# 373,915), which allowed communications between train stations and moving trains. Train accidents and collisions were causing great concern to both the public and the railways at the time. Wood's invention made it possible for trains to communicate with the station and with other trains so they knew precisely where they were at all times. This invention made train movements quicker and prevented countless accidents, collisions, and deaths. Yet this genius did not stop there. In 1900 Granville invented an Electric Incubator that was the predecessor to current machines that could incubate 50,000 eggs at a time. In the following three years he patented a series of advances in the development of Air Brakes and air brake design. Granville T. Woods attained great fame as a prolific inventor which moved mankind forward through exceptional innovations in communications, science, and technology. Inventions and contributions which improved the quality of life for all.

This ability to embrace the obstacle or obstacles, as it were; and utilize them as motivation and excel in spite of the situation was not and is not only attributed to the brothers. Negro women have pioneered and contributed to the progress of America and are of great importance in the Black Experience in general and in specific terms. In fact, the contributions of Black women aided in the progression of the status of all Women and Women's Rights. The founder of African-American literature was a Black woman. In 1773 poet Phyllis Wheatley became the first Negro to publish a book. The book was entitled "Poems on Various Subjects: Religious and Moral." Phyllis was brought from Africa to America in the year of 1761, recorded as being between seven and eight years of age. Without any formal education or even thought of access to a school, public or private, equipped merely with what she learned in her family and through observation, within 1 year & 4 months from her arrival in America, had mastered the English language. This to which she was an utter stranger to say the least, to such an impressive degree that when she read the most difficult parts of the Sacred Wings, it greatly astonished everyone. Wheatley is perhaps best remembered for her poem, "On Being Brought from Africa to America."

> "T'was mercy brought me from my pagan land,
> Taught my benighted soul to understand.
> That there's a God, that there's a Savior too.
> Once redemption I neather sought nor knew
> Some view our fable race with swornful eye,
> "Their color is a diabolic die"
> Remember, Christians, Negroes; black as cain.
> May be refined, and join the angelic train."

This great poem is explosive and profound in terms of Phyllis Wheatley's interpretation of the African Experience in America and America in general. Her writing bears note and has great meaning in terms of her experiencing life in Africa versus life in America at that time. It is rooted in her living, understanding, and experiencing both continents, both cultures; and yet, the ability to translate these cultures and concepts to published literature. Wheatley pioneered and literature. Negro women also pioneered in Business in Industry.

Sarah E. Goode was a businesswoman, and inventor, and industrial pioneer. Goode invented the Folding Cabinet Bed, a tremendous space saver which folded up against the wall into a cabinet. When folded up it could be used as a desk, complete with compartments. Goode's patent for the folding cabinet bed (U.S. Patent# 322,177), was approved in July of 1885 was the first to be obtained by an African-American woman. This opened the door to space management and the efficiency of the studio apartment.

The first African-American millionaire was a woman. Sarah Walker (1857-1919), the daughter of Louisiana sharecroppers and nick-named "Madame C.J." was the first woman; not only first Negro woman, the first female to sell products via mail order and to organize a nationwide membership of door-to-door Sales Representatives. Orphaned at seven, married and 14, widowed at 20, and was left an estate worth $2 million. Madame C.J. created hair care products for Black women. She also invented the Pressing Comb and Hair Conditioner for hair straightening. Both Madame C.J. and her inventions were of ground-breaking merit. She is best remembered as one of the first businesswomen of any race, creed, color, or continent to become a millionaire through her our own efforts. Hence the next time you beautiful ladies do your Perm, Press-n-Curl, or treat your hair; thank Madame C.J...

Of course we cannot fully explore and execute our text and message without acknowledging the "fore-mother" of Black America, the Honorable Harriet Tubman. Born Araminta Ross, Harriet Tubman was born into slavery in 1819 in Dorchester County, Maryland. Given the names of her parents, both held in slavery, she was purely of African ancestry. Raised under harsh conditions, and subjected to whippings even as a small child. At age 6, Araminta was considered to be able to work. Her master, as it were, Edward Brodas did not put her in the fields. He loaned her to a couple who used her to weave; she was beaten frequently and then given the job of checking the muskrat traps from which she caught measles. Upon her recovery she was returned to Brodas and then loaned to another couple who used her as a baby sitter. They whipped and returned her for eating a sugar cube. When she turned 11, as was the custom on all plantations, she started wearing a bright cotton bandanna around her head indicating that she was no longer a child. At the age of 12, Harriet was seriously injured by a blow to the head; curiously from a white overseer for her refusing to assist in tying up a man; a man who had attempted to escape his enslavement.

In 1844 at the age of 25, she married John Tubman, a free Black man, who unfortunately did not share her dream. He did believe in the task assigned to her by God. Harriet knew that she could be sold at any time and her marriage split apart. Harriet wanted to go North where they could live free without fear of separation. He did not want to leave and vowed to tell her master if she escaped. In 1849 Harriet escaped slavery, leaving her husband and master Brodas and his oppression, and made it to Philadelphia. Here, Harriet got a job where she saved her wages to help free slaves. Here, Harriet met William Still. Still was one of the Underground Railroad's busiest station masters. William Still was a free-born Black man from Pennsylvania who could read and write. He interviewed runaway slaves and recorded their names and experiences. Still published in this book in 1872 under the title "Underground Railroad" which describes many of Harriet Tubman's efforts.

With the assistance of William Still and other members of the Philadelphia Anti-Slavery Society, Harriet learned of the Underground Railroad. And in 1850, Harriet helped her first slave escape to the freedom of the North. In 1850, Harriet was made an official "Conductor" of the Underground Railroad. This meant that she knew all of the routes to free territory and had to take an oath of silence. By the winter of 1852, Tubman had led so many people from the bondage and oppression of the South, the slaves called the North, "The land of Egypt," to freedom; she became known as Moses. She was also known by plantation owners and acknowledged by a bounty of $40,000 posted. The State of Maryland posted a $12,000 reward for her capture. Tubman worked closely with famed abolitionist John Brown, who was so overwhelmed by her successful efforts and intelligence that he called her General Tubman. She reportedly missed the raid on Harper's Ferry only because of illness. Harriet's work in the Underground Railroad was ending by December 1860. She made her last rescue trip to Maryland, bringing seven slaves to Canada. In 10 years she worked as a conductor on the Underground Railroad, Harriet managed to rescue over 300 slaves. She made 19 trips and never lost a passenger on the way. For Harriet's own safety, her friends took her to Canada.

Amazingly, the Underground Railroad was not the only significant contribution of Harriet Tubman. In 1861 Harriet returned to the United States from living in

Canada and assisted the Union in the Civil War. She even managed to get around the numerous Bounties on her head. In 1861 the Civil War had begun and the Union was enlisting all men as soldiers and any women who wanted to join as cooks and nurses. Tubman enlisted in the Union Army as a "Contraband" nurse in Hilton Head, South Carolina and for a time serving at Fortress Monroe, where Jefferson Davis would be later imprisoned. Contrabands were Blacks who the Union Army helped to escape from the Southern compounds. Harriet nursed the sick and wounded back to health and when the Army sent her to another hospital in Florida, she found White soldiers and contrabands dying off like sheep. She treated her patients, Black and White; with medicine from roots and amazingly never caught the deadly diseases the wounded soldiers would carry.

During the summer of 1863, Harriet begin working with Colonel James Montgomery as a scout. She put together a group of spies who kept Montgomery informed on slaves who may be interested in joining the Union Army. After Tubman and her spies completed the groundwork, she helped Montgomery organize the Combahee River Raid. The purpose of the raid was to harass whites and rescue freed blacks. They were successful in attacking the rebel outposts and gathering almost 500 slaves. Almost all of the freed slaves joined the Union Army. The United States Government did not pay Tubman's military pension until the 1890's in the amount of $20 per month. In 1869 Tubman return home to Auburn and married Nelson Davis, whom she met while guiding and a group of black soldiers in South Carolina and they shared a calm and peaceful 19 year marriage and until he died. Before Harriet died in 1913, she gave her home to the Methodist Episcopal Zion Church to help the elderly. Harriet was buried with military rights in Fort Hill Cemetery, a short drive from her home. Harriet Tubman lived a life of relentless dedication to freedom and liberty and continues to be the greatest female African American ancestor to date. Understand that she could have lived reasonably comfortable in Philadelphia after escaping slavery and securing a job; but went beyond her personal her comfort zone and success and went about God's business.

Many of the families, both prominent and otherwise who populate the North today are the children of slaves. Saved, blessed, and delivered by God, facilitated by way of the Underground Railroad to freedom and opportunity. These former used and abused slaves secured jobs was paid actual currency and not chitterlings, beatings, and barn sleeping accommodations; the compensation package of slavery. They endeavored to establish new lives in the North in the early urban centers of Boston, Cincinnati, and Philadelphia where free blacks were living. Equipped only with freedom and the desire for opportunity and progress, the newly freed Negro was ready to take an active and equal part in America. The nectar-like air of freedom was indeed sweet for the Negro and equal rights and opportunities were supposed to be inclusive of free life. However "Free Life" was no crystal stair. You see, the Emancipation Proclamation and the Amendments to the Constitution of the United States of America mandated freedom and citizenship to the Negro with all the rights and privileges therein. Yet the Negro only received half of their deal with the United States. Yes there was freedom; legally, but there was no economic, educational, or social resources to establish communities, self-sufficiency, or prosperity. True free life.

The United States refused to compensate the newly freed Negro for the centuries of exploitation and free labor by extending the "True" rights of citizenship and fulfilling the Lincoln Plan of 40 Acres and a Mule; thereby giving the Negro the ability to make the transformation and growth from that of dependency to that of independence. To be allowed to evolve from a strictly labor class to a competitive, self sustaining race of people. Instead of assisting the Negro by making provisions for economic resources which were absolutely vital to the growth and ultimate independence of any community; the Negro was released to make his own way. To "Fend for Himself," as it were. The Negro was not only unequipped with the tools to facilitate progress with new their freedom, but was completely unprepared for the laws, acts, and treatment which were implemented specifically to restrain Negro progress. Within an era which should have reshaped the social, economic, and political operations of the United States; the period following slavery left the Negro in limbo, living between slavery and freedom.

This period is historically acknowledged and addressed as, "The Reconstruction Era." The Reconstruction Era is defined as the period immediately following the Civil War during which the United States engaged to rebuild the South physically, politically, socially, and economically. This truly important period in American history from 1865 to 1877 was one of both triumph and tragedy for the Negro; but also another missed opportunity for America to correct or at least pay for its past indiscretions. This period gave birth to Negro presence and participation in American politics. Serving as elected officials working towards equality, democracy, and human rights, a period which also gave birth to various acts, legislation, and codes that were engaged to limit Negro Civil rights, human rights, and progress. The first plan presented and which began the Reconstruction Era was The Ten Percent Plan by President Lincoln in December 1863 which stated that after 10% of a Confederate State's Pre-Civil War voters take an oath of loyalty to the United States Constitution; then it's citizens could elect a new State Government and apply for re-admission to the Union of the United States of America.

The 10% percent plan also required that the States amend their Constitutions to abolish Slavery. Congress felt that Lincoln's Reconstruction Plan was too soft and moved to enact stronger legislation. In late 1864 Congress passed the Wade-Davis Bill, which required that 50% of a State's voters declare loyalty to the United States Constitution before the State could create a new government and that this new government recognize freed people as equal citizens before the law. President Lincoln indirectly vetoed the Wade-Davis Bill by leaving it unendorsed until Congress adjourned in late March 1865. Earlier in that legislative session, Congress approved the 13th Amendment which constitutionally ended slavery. This was officially ratified in December 1865. However, by the end of the Congressional session in March 1865 Congress had moved to establish the Bureau of Refugees, Freedmen and Abandoned Lands, known as the Freedman's Bureau, a relief agency to help former slaves primarily.

The assassination of Abraham Lincoln and its effect on the post Civil War Era and Reconstruction was tremendously significant. President Lincoln's assassination on Sunday, April 15, 1865 ended the chances of Negro compensation, but it also gave way to the Presidency of the Vice-President Andrew Johnson, a poor white man from Tennessee with harbored hatred for the Southern slave owning aristocracy and for the Negro. Immediately after Lincoln's assassination, in May of 1865 Johnson began unveiling Reconstruction proclamations far softer than Lincoln's. Johnson pardoned all Southern whites excluding Confederate leaders and individuals with wealth which surpassed $20,000. They would have to personally apply for the Presidential pardon. He appointed provisional Governors and required that to rejoin the Union, the States merely needed to abolish Slavery and denounce secession and the Confederate War debt. After the rebellious States met these "requirements," they were considered "Reconstructed." Further, Johnson ordered the abandoned plantations be returned to their former slave holding owners.

One specific tragedy was that of the lands on the Sea Islands of South Carolina which was abandoned early in the Civil War by the Confederates as the United States Army approached South Carolina. Freed Negroes immediately lobbied for ownership of the land, insisting that it was rightfully theirs following generations of forced servitude and oppression. The United States Government instead, implemented the Port Royal Experiment, in which freed people who labored in the abandoned Sea Islands were paid as wage workers. Eventually General William T. Sherman issued Special Order 15, which officially gave the land to the freed people. President Johnson, however, rescinded Special Order 15, and the Sea Island was handed back to its original inhumane, slave owners.

INVESTMENT IN AMERICA

Although representatives from the Freedman Bureau initially refused to comply with Johnson's directive; he ultimately sent Federal troops to force the return of numerous lands and plantations. The United States Government's failure to redistribute land was the major mistake of Reconstruction. America missed a second opportunity to reconcile its indiscretions.

* * *

CHAPTER V

NATION DEFINING DECADES

Due to the policies and outright insensitivity of President Johnson, the worst President that America has endured; particularly Negro America. America's greatness and perfection as a Nation was derailed. Abraham Lincoln had not only saved the Union that we now know as the United States of America; but also engaged the challenge of righting the wrongs of America, and establishing its greatness as a Nation. The now President Johnson essentially gave the South right back to the Confederates. No punishment; instead policies which the Confederate States; the advocates of Secession from the Union and of Slavery, were greatly encouraged and promptly rejoined the "Union." Returning to their properties, plantations and power.

This comfort level facilitated by the United States Government by order of President Johnson allowed these former Confederate States to enact "Black Codes;" the next nightmare for the Negro. Black Codes were defined as legal statutes that curtailed the rights of Negroes in the early years of Reconstruction in the United States. Black Codes were instituted by the Southern Legislative bodies in 1865 and 1866 in order to circumvent the Civil Rights Legislation of Reconstruction and regain control and power over the 4 million newly emancipated Negroes. Just as Slave Code Legislation allowed the inhumanity which endorsed and permitted slavery, Black Code Legislation allowed the continuation of inhumane treatment. Just as the Slave Codes denied and Negroes any legal status besides that of being property, Black Codes defined Black People as legally subordinate to White People.

Under Black Codes interracial marriages were banned and Negroes could be forced to sign yearly contracts. They limited in the occupations they could pursue and the types of jobs Negroes could get and the property Negroes could own. Mississippi and South Carolina proceeded to pass laws in 1865 which forced Black men and women to work or face imprisonment, which the States of Alabama and Louisiana followed shortly thereafter and by 1866 all of the States of the former Confederacy, except North Carolina, had enacted laws that echoed the Slave Codes. Further, these States approved legislation that permitted the imprisonment or hiring out of "vagrants." A "vagrant" and/or "vagrancy" was defined as **being a Black Man or Woman who was unemployed or possessing no contract with a White employer**. In many situations, freed man and women returned to work for their former masters or on nearby plantations. Others labored as wage workers; even skilled workers and Artisans, because of exorbitant licensing fees were also forced into wage working segment of the Code. Others engaged in what appeared to be a good deal for the Black farmer; but was in reality another mechanism of servitude; "Share-cropping."

Share-cropping was a situation in which the farmer (the sharecropper) was a farmer/tenant who gives a share of his crops to the plantation owner/landlord in lieu of rent. The sharecropper was often severely taken advantage of with little to no recourse. When resorting to the Freedman's Bureau whose primary role was to mediate such disputes and fight such abuses usually sided with the former slave mastering plantation owners. Forcing them to fight for themselves or as many did; depend on the mercy and good will of their former masters. Sharecropping and its treatment prevailed for years throughout the Southern States. Although sharecropping began as a way to maximize land by cultivating and extension of credit in an economically challenged, poor credit region, it relegated many freed people to a state of virtual peonage; which often put the Negro in situations materially worse than slavery.

Throughout the Reconstruction period Blacks utilized any rights they could, and truly exercised the right to vote; almost unanimously voting for Republican candidates in the 1866 Congressional elections. Blacks began to participate in government and in politics. Submerged in oppression for economics, politically used or ignored; the Negro was a participate in the governing of America. Primarily due to large Negro voter turnout and because Congress banned many former Confederates from politics, the Republican Party won control of many

NATION DEFINING DECADES

Southern Constitutional Conventions. Of the 1,000 Republican Delegates to the Constitutional Conventions throughout the South, 265 were Black. Black presence in government was greatest in State and local government. P.B.S. Pitchback became the first Negro Governor in the history of the United States. He was also elected to both the U.S. Senate and the United States House of Representatives. Hiram R. Revels was the son of slaves who became a minister, an educator, and the first Negro in the United States Senate. In total, 16 Negroes served in the U.S. Congress during Reconstruction.

Reconstruction inspired deep resentment among Southern whites and former Confederates who were quite bitter about losing the war, their power, and facing their challenges to be fair. They believed that white Republicans were indeed, "race traitors," and objected to the exorbitant taxes that Republicans enacted to pay for Reconstruction. The Southern whites wanted one thing; to restore "White Rule." In the prevailing situation this could be accomplished only through white collective action. The Southern whites convinced whites to vote Democrat in States with white majorities. This was enough to eliminate Republican rule. By 1871 Democrats had taken back Tennessee, Georgia, Virginia, and North Carolina.

In other States where continued Republican rule was dependent upon interracial relations, white Democrats went about the business of convincing Negroes not to vote through violence, employment intimidation, ["If you vote, don't come back to work"], and physical brutality and intimidation from the Worlds first official Terrorists; The Ku Klux Klan. I introduced the term terrorist because that is precisely what the organization was; a Terrorist Operation. In fact, often led by the most prominent whites in the community. The Klu Klux Klan was said to be originally the radical wing of the Democratic Party in the Reconstruction Era with the mission to win back white power and control over the South and the Negro.

The end of the Reconstruction Era was officially over in 1877 through the Compromise of 1877 However, by 1877 more than 600,000 Negroes had enrolled in Elementary Schools throughout the South. The Freedman's Bureau had founded over 4,000 schools, including Howard University in Washington, D.C.. The compromise was the result of the Presidential Election of 1876 in which Republican Rutherford B. Hayes and Democrat Samuel J. Tilden were virtually deadlocked. Tilden won the popular vote, but Republicans had control of South Carolina, Florida, and Louisiana; giving them control over the Electoral College. However, each party in these controlling States and competing Electors and Congress had to decide the Presidency. The incumbent Hayes, appointed an electoral commission which, by one more Republican than Democratic, declared him the winner.

The Democrats and Republicans worked out a deal, in which the Democrats would concede the White House and exchange for home rule in the critical aforementioned States. The remaining U.S. Military presence in South Carolina, Florida, and Louisiana departed. Republican rule crumbled and the Democrats had taken back the South in the process. Although it wasn't until the 1890's that the re-establishment of power was to be complete; whites created an excellent ally to facilitate and exploit power over the Negro. His name was **_Jim Crow_**. _Jim Crow_ embodied, perpetuated, and advocated what was "The Supremacist Manifesto." To keep Negro people down was the purpose of and gave birth to Jim Crow and its inhumane implementation.

Jim Crow is defined as a system of laws and customs that enforced racial segregation and discrimination throughout the United States, particularly in the South, from the late 19th century to the 1960's. Signs reading "Whites Only" or "Colored" hang over water fountains and the doors to rest rooms in restaurants, movie theaters, and other public places. This, in cooperation with segregation caused the Negro; specifically in the South to endure discrimination in employment, health care, and housing and were often denied their Constitutional Right to Vote. Ultimately, whether by law or by custom, these intentional obstacles set to prevent the bringing of the Negro to equal status went by the name Jim Crow.

Jim Crow was born in 1877 following the end of Reconstruction. I have been unable to specifically document how and why this name and term came to capture, embody, and define the hatred, inhumanity and discrimination of the Southern States of America. Originally Jim Crow was the name of a character in "minstrelsy," which consisted of white performers in "Black Face" using Negro stereotypes in their songs, dances and overall performance. This was the American vernacular for the most popular entertainment of the 19th century. It was the perpetual offspring, of Black Codes, Slave Codes, and the many other laws justifying discrimination, humiliation, and continued oppression of the Negro. The first and most controversial acts of Jim Crow legislation came from the transportation industry.

A law passed in New Orleans in 1890 mandated separate railroad cars for Negro and White passengers. This was soon followed by similar regulations in other Cities and States. The "laws," ostensibly written to protect both races, were endorsed on a federal level when the United States Supreme Court ruled in the litigation of Plessy vs. Ferguson in 1896 that "Separate but Equal" accommodations on Louisiana's railroads were Constitutional. This monumental ruling led to

NATION DEFINING DECADES

legalized segregation in education, public parks, libraries and in other laws which were indirect or non-race specific in its wording; but targeted for the enemy; the Negro. The non-race specific acts such as the passing of the polling taxes and literacy tests administered with informal loopholes and trick questions which were utilized to disqualify nearly all Negroes from voting. For example, although more than 130,000 Negroes were registered to vote in Louisiana in 1896, a mere 1,342 of the voting rolls voted in 1904.

Jim Crow extended to deny private, public, and civil rights to Negroes. Businesses often refused to serve Negroes, most white homeowners would not sell or rent to Negroes, and the humiliating denial of social respect; addressing Black men as "boy" and having an expectation of deference to whites; made life quite difficult. These aforementioned factors accompanied by dismal economic conditions and employment opportunities, lynchings, the Ku Klux Klan, and drastically unbalanced segregated education for the children compelled many Blacks to vacate the South and the shameful Jim Crow Era. This exodus is historically known as "The Great Northern Migration" of the 1920's, 1930's, and 1940's.

Referenced as one of the largest domestic migrations in the history of North America, this period of Negro relocation and struggle against Jim Crow was a very significant period. This period would also engulf America in a national economic struggle; The Great Depression. This Great Depression brought with it a period of economic hardship throughout the United States that landed with particularly damaging effects on Blacks. However for Blacks, this depression of great proportion in American economic, social, and political history began long before the Stock Market of 1929, which launched the depression. In the 1920's Southern Black farmers and sharecroppers endured the devastating effect of the boll weevil on their cotton harvest. They also suffered a dramatic decrease in farming pricing which proceeded World War I as President Woodrow Wilson lifted agricultural price supports. Further, the government canceled all wartime orders. What is interesting is that this period of national devastation; this Great Depression period, and the poverty and suffering during this depression because of the Stock Market Crash of 1929. Because this "crash," was no accident.

The Stock Market Crash of 1929 was scientifically engineered by International Bankers and major financing players in Europe and the United States to take profits and to exercise power. They held the power to move and devastate a market, and economy, a Nation. Among the most powerful and influential were J. Pierpont Morgan; an International Financing, Banking, Political, and Power Brokering genius. An associate of the outrageously powerful Rothchilds global dynasty, J. P.

Morgan was instrumental in pushing the United States into World War I to protect his loans to the British Government. He was the chief engineer of the panic of 1907, merely to make a point and advocate the mission of the insiders to lobby for creating a Central Banking System for the United States in order to supposedly strip Wall Street and International Bankers of their power over economies. This led to the successful passing of the Federal Reserve Act in 1913 and the birth of the Federal Reserve System, the most powerful entity today; worldwide.

The Crash of 1929 was the profit-taking or "cash-out of the International Bankers and insiders whom the Federal Reserve System was developed to neutralize. Leaving the gold standard for one of paper currency and promising no more boom or bust economic cycles, but steady growth and prosperity. Utilizing a Central Bank to control inflation and deflation appeared to be the perfect fit. After working well for a while, between 1923 and 1929, the Federal Reserve expanded (inflated) the money supply by 62%. Most of this new money was used to bid the stock market up by great numbers. Following the meeting between Norman Montagu, Governor of the Bank of England and Andrew Mellon, United States Secretary of the Treasury; the Federal Reserve Board reversed its easy money policy and began raising the discount rate. The inflating of the money supply balloon was about to explode.

On October 24, 1929, the beef hit the grill. As described by William Bryan in *The United States Unresolved Monetary Problems,:*

"When everything was ready, the New York financiers started calling 24-hour broker call loans. This meant that the stockbrokers and the customers had to dump their stocks in the market in order to pay their loans. This naturally collapsed the stock market and brought a Banking collapse all over the country because the banks not owned by the oligarchy were heavily involved in broker call claims at the time, and Bank runs soon exhausted their coin and currency and they had to close. The Federal Reserve system would not come to their aid, although they were instructed under the law to maintain an elastic currency."

As the investing public including most stockbrokers and bankers, the United States economy took a tremendous hit in the crash, but not the insiders. They were either out of the market or had shorted their stocks so they made enormous profits as the Dow Jones plummeted. I took the liberty of going into some detail with regard to the depression because of its impact on Negro life in America at that time; and to highlight its impact on overall life in America, on all people, and provide a picture of the State of the Union economically, socially, and politically

NATION DEFINING DECADES

at that point in time. For it is important to remember that while Communities and Races and Religions have their respective struggles; there is a bigger picture of "Macro" level contexts that is taken place as the "Micro" level struggles continue. The depression period is interesting because it was a period which introduced the United States to poverty. Poverty to the general population of America; not just the Negro.

Simultaneously, the Great Migration was taking place and many Negroes abandoned their working properties and farming and relocated to the cities of the North. Unfortunately, the low-wage employment that they found in the urban centers forced them to reside in cramped, low rent dwellings and low quality of life. Many of these centers evolved into our present-day ghettos. The migration also prompted dramatically increased activity and support for the Ku Klux Klan in the North; unprecedented support. The depression only made matters worse; economically as well as in race relations. By 1932 roughly half of the African American workers in New York, Pittsburgh, Chicago, Detroit, and Philadelphia were without jobs, and nearly 33% of African American families were receiving some form of government assistance. Yet the white unemployment rate was much lower. The number of lynchings of African Americans; rather, the documented number of lynchings increased from seven in 1929 to 20 in 1930 to 24 in 1933, which was the worse year of the economic collapse.

The early 1900's was indeed a period of hostility, poverty, and outright racism in a still developing America. It was a period which would help define America and further define the Negro resolve and contribution. Collective action, militant activity, and persistence were the weapons used to combat this problem. This response to the inhumane treatment, brought the greatest, political, and racial intellectual argument and debate of this critical period and for periods to follow. The debate of embracing and adhering to second-class citizenship and treatment vs. the rightful advocation of equal rights and treatment under the Constitutional Rule of Law. The debate between Booker T. Washington and the great W. E. B. DuBois; genius. Booker T. Washington believed and advocated that Negroes should except second-class status and strive to obtain industrial training and jobs which would eventually facilitate assimilation and equal treatment in America. DuBois strongly believed and advocated that the American Negro was due every right that was granted to any free American; political, social, and civil. Further, that protesting and pushing for equality and due rights; not the acceptance of inequality and limited rights; were the answer to the great plight of Negro life in America.

Tuskegee Institute, (now Tuskegee University) was chartered by the Alabama

State Legislature to repay Negro voters for their support. In February 1881, the Alabama Legislature voted to set aside or "escrow" in today's terms, $2,000 per year to capitalize a normal State School for Negroes in Tuskegee, Alabama. After searching and being unsuccessful in finding a white principal (quiet as it was kept); Booker T. Washington was the first principal hired at Tuskegee and was well supported by white public officials and philanthropist in the North as well as the South. They greatly appreciated his ideals and advocacy of embracing second-class treatment and Tuskegee University was well liked by whites.

Tuskegee Institute was of great benefit to the United States and the world; for it gave America the Tuskegee Airmen, and gave the world Dr. George Washington Carver. Agricultural genius, inventor, educator whose innovations, of which; if I could offer just one; "Peanut Butter," changed the world. Peanut Butter addressed and continues to address hunger and malnutrition issues; worldwide. George Washington Carver resigned from his teaching post at Iowa State College of Agriculture and Mechanical Arts (now Iowa State University) to accept an invitation from Booker T. to head the Agricultural Department at Tuskegee which lacked facilities or funds for an Agricultural Department; consisting of a barn, a cow, and a few chickens. He believed in Booker T. and rejected several offers from large, well funded agricultural departments of Universities to dedicate his knowledge to invent, teach, and help the Negro cause.

Tuskegee Institute was also the place where one of the most inhumane medical experiments to date; the Tuskegee Syphilis Experiment. The Tuskegee Syphilis Experiment, conducted by the United States Public Health Service and Tuskegee Institute began in 1932 and was originally planned to last one year. The purpose of this widely condemned "experiment" was to study the natural course of syphilis in which U.S. public health officials withheld treatment from 600 African American males, of which, 399 were infected with syphilis.

William Edward Burghardt DuBois, born February 23, 1868 in Great Barrington, Massachusetts and died August 27, 1963 in Accra, Ghana; Black America's top public intellectual throughout his adult life, founded the Niagara Movement in 1905 with William Trotter. The Niagara Movement, labeled militant, was a specific response to Booker T. Washington's accommodating, tip-toe approach to racial justice and equality. Booker T. did not truly address racial justice and equality. Although not long lasting (1905 to 1910), the Niagara Movement was an important step in the birth and evolution of protests and movements from Negro America. In 1903 DuBois published his first literary contribution, *The Souls of Black Folk*; which many have called the most significant book ever written by an African-American. In this great undertaking he identified **"The Color Line"** as the 20th Century's primary problem, and dismissed the accommodationism advocated by Washington who claimed that," the agitation of questions of social equality is the extremists folly," and in his Atlanta Compromise, urged the Negro to replace the quest for civil and political equality with focusing on agriculture, mechanics, and domestic service.

DuBois acknowledged and was fervent in his advocation of the greatness in the Negro and the due right of equal treatment. He recognized the existence of and presented, *The Talented Tenth*, a small number of well educated Negro professionals such as Paul Lawrence Dunbar; Poet, Charles W. Chestnut; Novelist, Henry O. Tanner; Artist and Painter. In an essay in 1903 as he identified them as being a part of the advanced representatives of the race and of what this race brings to the table. The Talented Tenth developed and propagated a new ideal of racial assertiveness which was embraced by the physicians, bankers, preachers, educators, dentists, morticians and business owners. They comprised the bulk of the Negro American affluent and influential; some 10,000 men and women out of total population of 10 million and was the catalyst of the Harlem Renaissance, the most significant period of Negro American Evolution in every area.

The visionary DuBois also knew that the goal was righteous, yet an adjusted approach was needed. A middle of the road undertaking, if you will, was the best solution. A less "militant," yet more effective plan and approach. Enter the National Association for the Advancement of Colored People (NAACP). Founded February 12, 1909, the NAACP has been unquestionably vital and a key component in improving the legal, economic, and educational rights of Negroes. Accepting and uniting the white and Jewish philanthropic support which characterized Booker T. Washington's accommodationist organizations with the demand for racial justice delivered by DuBois's Niagara Movement, the NAACP forged a middle of the road approach to interracial cooperation to obtain equality

The NAACP was formed in response to the Springfield Race Riot of 1908, the capital of the State of Illinois and the birthplace of Abraham Lincoln. Outraged and ashamed of the violence that was inflicted upon Negroes, a group of white liberals spearheaded by Oswald Garrison Villard and Mary Ovington White, both descendents of abolitionists, issued a call for a meeting to discuss racial justice. 60 people endorsed the call; only 7 of which were Black which included W. E. B. DuBois, Ida B. Wells, and Mary Church-Terrell, and was released to the public on the Centennial of Lincoln's birth. Echoing the focus of DuBois' all Black Niagara Movement, the NAACP's stated goal was to secure the rights granted and **"said to be"** guaranteed in the 13th, 14th, and 15th Amendments to the Constitution of the

United States of America, which promised to end Slavery, provide Equal Protection under the Law, and complete Adult Male Suffrage.

    The NAACP established its National Headquarters in New York City and named a Board of Directors and a President, Moorfield Storey, a White Constitutional Law Attorney and former President of the American Bar Association. The only Negro among the organizations executive leadership was DuBois, who was made Director of Publications and Research. In 1910 DuBois was very busy; speaking, writing and establishing the official journal of the NAACP, ***The Crisis***. This great publication became the voice of the Negro struggle and the Harlem Renaissance, as DuBois published the great writings of Langston Hughes, Countee Cullen and many other great Black American literary figures. 1910 was in itself, was a very busy year:

* United States Total Population   -----   93.4 Million
* United States Negro Population   -----   9.8 Million **(10% of U.S. Total)**
* Negroes in South Carolina obtain complete control of the State Republican Convention
* The National Urban League is established
* W. C. Handy publishes *Memphis Blues*
* There were **67 "known"** lynchings of African Americans
* A Lawsuit was brought in the U.S. Circuit Court to compel the City of Annapolis, Maryland to register Negro voters. Annapolis, through a City Ordinance, had attempted to nullify the 15th Amendment.
* W. E. B. DuBois and Booker T. Washington clash when Washington declared in a speech to The Anti-Slavery and Aborigines Protection Society that the condition of Negroes in the United States was being satisfactorily resolved. DuBois issue an *"Appeal to Europe"* which bitterly challenged that assertion.
* Jack Johnson, the first African American Heavyweight Champion, knocks out James "The Great White Hope" Jeffries to retain the Title.
* The secret meeting at Jekyl Island with Senator Nelson Aldrich, Henry P. Davidson of J.P. Morgan & Company, Frank A. Vandelip, President of the Rockefeller owned National City Bank, A. Piatt Andrew, Assistant Secretary of the Treasury, Benjamin Strong of Morgan Bankers Trust Company, and Paul Warburg to create an American Central Bank which would become **The Federal Reserve**.
* ***The Pittsburgh Courier*** begins publishing.
* President Taft nominates Robert Terrell to be a Judge in the Municipal Court of the District of Columbia.

NATION DEFINING DECADES

From W. E. B. DuBois and the birth of the NAACP to James Weldon Johnson and its growth to Thurgood Marshall in its greatest triumph; (the victory achieved in *Brown vs. The Board of Education*, the decision which overturned *Plessy vs. Ferguson*); the work and contributions of the NAACP and the icons they brought to the table are above reproach.

* * *

CHAPTER VI

A PEOPLE ON A MISSION

There are some who attribute the success of the NAACP and Black progress to white liberals and to the Black alliance with Jews. There is truth in the former; yet to a lesser degree in the latter. This "alliance" is overstated and factually incorrect. From the beginning of this "Alliance" in the early 1900's, the Jews kept their problems and the problems of Negroes in perspective. Jewish problems came first; and the Jews did not truly identify with the Negro. The Negro did not receive equal Love; or at least loyalty. The Jews; fleeing persecution in Europe in the first and second decades of the 20th century, entered the United States of America and endured the same world of separate but equal and Jim Crowism as the Negro. The majority of the Jews were poor, liberal, and alone. A few were sympathetic to Negro problems and united with Negroes to fight prejudice. However, although their intentions may have been noble, the Jews who helped Negroes, and to fully engage the subject, as well as the abolitionists; who were of great help, were unsuccessful in resolutions to the plight as it continues, is due to basic philosophical mistakes in the understanding of and/or in the implementation of their efforts to help.

The mistake in the abolitionist effort was that they did not either understand or ignored the fact that Slavery was an economic issue; which it was, and therefore should be treated as one. They interpreted and addressed the Institution of Slavery as a moral issue, and thought that abolishment would be the answer. This misinterpretation of the big picture of Slavery, focusing only on morality, made abolitionists focus on engaging the "right & wrong of it all," not the Economics of it all. They continued to purchase and utilize slave produced items, such as tobacco products, cotton goods, table foods, alcoholic beverages, silver and gold jewelry, and Iron products; as opposed to boycotting them. You see, by not engaging the Institution of Slavery as an economic issue, the abolitionist; consciously or unconsciously supported Slavery and therefore flawed their efforts to combat it.

The mistake in the efforts of individual Jews, consciously or unconsciously; to help the Negro plight was in their encouraging the Negro to do something that Jews themselves did not want to do. Assimilate into the general white population and culture of America. Jews were helpful and loaned support to the quest for Negroes to obtain Civil Rights and Voting rights. However these "rights"; which were in all due respect, important in principal, facilitated the perception of making Negroes equal and self-sufficient. Yet, when in fact, these accomplishments could not and still can not significantly change the power base and wealth base of Negroes. What is even more tragic, is that this "Socioeconomic Alliance" between Jews and Negroes did not emphasize Negroes learning and implementing the self-sufficiency skills and strategies mastered by the Jews.

In the 1920's and 1930's, Negroes returned the favor; if you will, by aligning with Jews against Religious bigotry and oppression. The alliance was beneficial to both groups but mainly to Jews by far, and presented a common front against some common Conservative adversaries. The alliance assisted Negroes in obtaining access to high levels of Government and some access to the "Corporate World." In return for Jewish support, Blacks gave Jews the *Gold Card*, unencumbered and unmitigated access to every aspect of Black American life, culture, skills, and society. The Jews established neighborhood businesses that were set up which flourished and triumphed exclusively from Black patronage. They advised Black leaders on public policy matters. The Jews built entire industries and great wealth around the talents that Blacks possessed, controlled, or owned, such as professional sports, music, and entertainment.

The NAACP and other African American organizations and leaders were advised to quietly pursue social integration and seek upward mobility within the structure and mainstream American society. Negro leadership believed that once integration was accomplished, Civil Rights would accompany this achievement; quality of life would have to get better for all Negroes. After all, this strategy worked for the Jews. However, as American society began to soften its virulent anti-Semitism of the 1940's, Jews used their new found mobility to secure wealth and power for themselves. The "alliance" began to break as Blacks became increasingly disenchanted with their lack of progress and stagnant socioeconomic condition, and as the economic and social fortunes and power of Jews and Blacks began to diverge, the relationship became more paternalistic.

Blacks outside of the traditional Civil Rights organizations became convinced that the only way to change the plight and immoral treatment was for Blacks to take complete economic and political control of their communities, institutions, and lives. Growing weary of the promises of progress and equality yet none taking place; more decisive action was required. Many expressed Anti-White feelings which alarmed and threatened the status quo. By way of protest, symbols, and riots; Black America, or at least a significant segment thereof, informed the United States of America that they had lost faith in the system and its' justice. They sought other alternative Negro leadership and methods and were determined to obtain equal treatment. Clearly, more aggressive strategies and measures were in order. More aggressive leadership from individuals and organizations specifically dedicated to equality.

Leaders such as A. Phillip Randolph., founder and President of the Brotherhood of Sleeping Car Porters (PSCP), editor and cofounder of *The Messenger*, and architect of the March on Washington Movement in 1941, which led to the establishment of the Fair Employment Practices Committee (FEPC). A. Philip Randolph spent his life as a Labor and Equal Rights leader and made a tremendous contribution to Black American progress in very real terms. He successfully organized and represented the Pullman Porters 10,000 members and fought, battled and finally negotiated with the President and Congress to amend the Railway Labor Act. This great accomplishment was cheered and celebrated by Blacks and progressive Whites nationwide. Because the purpose of this text is to teach and not to preach; this hurdle, this important contribution must be somewhat detailed in explanation, in order to communicate its impact on Black employment rights and on Black economic life. The Pullman Company, although founded just shortly after the Civil War, by the 1920's had become the single largest employer of Blacks in the United States. The Pullman Porters completely consisted of Black Men. Further, most of the Pullman Porters were College graduates who enjoyed much respect in their communities, yet at work they were subjected to unfair and discriminatory practices. For ten years, in spite of intimidation attempts and firings, Randolph kept the Brotherhood members inspired and completely unified until their Union was officially recognized by the Pullman Company in 1935.

Randolph was also the catalyst in the success of desegregating the United

States Armed Forces and Defense Industries. In 1940 Randolph along with Walter White of the National Association for the Advancement of Colored People and T. Arnold Hill of the National Urban League, urged President Franklin D. Roosevelt to desegregate the Armed Forces (Army, Navy, Air Force, and Marines) and the jobs in the defense industry before World War II. Following unsuccessful attempts to arrive to an agreement with the President Roosevelt, Randolph began planning a March on Washington by the Brotherhood of Sleeping Car Porters and others to demand, "the right to equality in working and fighting for our country." With a mass demonstration planned and people eager to protest, President Roosevelt issued Executive Order 8002 which prohibited discrimination in the growing and prosperous defense industry and established the Fair Employment Practices Committee to investigate breaches of the order.

However, Randolph did not rest on his victories, he continued to push to accomplish his other and yet greater goal; the desegregation of the United States Armed Forces. When President Harry S. Truman instituted a peacetime draft, A. Philip Randolph told him, "This time the Negro will not take a Jim Crow draft lying down." And in July 1948 President Truman signed Executive Order 9981, finally ending the historic segregation of Negro soldiers. Another factor in helping to influence President Truman's decision was the performance of and contribution of the Tuskegee Airmen, of the segregated United States Air Force in World War II that broke records in military service. The 332nd fighter group, which was formed and excelled despite set up barriers, the Airmen preserved and overcame, and their work was outstanding. Assigned mostly to Italy, their fighter planes escorted bombers on their way to Europe, and in 1,578 missions and 15,552 sorties, they never lost a bomber. They destroyed or damaged 409 enemy planes. They even sank a German Destroyer in Trieste Harbor, marking the first time a vessel of that size and capability to have been sunk simply by machine gun fire. Another group of distinction; the Red Ball Express, an all Negro World War II trucking operation, whose motto was "We Deliver." The Red Ball Express consisted of 8,000 drivers which successfully delivered ammunition, gas, food, medicine, injured soldiers, etc.; and against all odds and danger; always delivered.

Randolph continued further in Civil Rights, meeting with President Dwight D. Eisenhower to push for faster school integration in wake of the *Brown vs. Board of Education* decision that was an important part of President Lyndon Baines Johnson signing the Civil Rights Act of 1964 and awarding Randolph with the Presidential Medal of Freedom. Asa Philip Randolph was the phototype of focused and effective leadership which got results and helped to prepare the path for one of the greatest advocates ever; the Honorable Reverend Dr. Martin Luther King, Jr.

A PEOPLE ON A MISSION

The Reverend Dr. Martin Luther King, Jr. aggressive, non-violent, fighting without striking a blow, righteous leadership was and continues to be the most prolific representation of God's principles and commandments living and manifesting in a man since Jesus Christ. He forced the blood of conscious, equity, and fairness into the veins of an ever-growing powerful, yet immoral racist nation. Please understand that the Reverend Dr. Martin Luther King, Jr. was not assassinated just because of what he was doing for Negroes; but for what he was doing for all poor and disenfranchised people. Therefore his greatness and legacy belongs to the World because righteousness and equal treatment is a right, a God-given human right; worldwide.

In Dr. King's academic studies at Morehouse College, Crozer Theological Seminary, and Boston University, he was fascinated and empowered by the works and teachings on non-violent protest of another great and righteous man; India's great leader, The Honorable Mohandas Ghandi, next on the list of the great leaders in all of history and mankind. Truly leading by example. Leading through righteousness, purpose, and sacrifice; a natural model from which Dr. King could draw from. Martin Luther king, Jr. studied, embraced, and utilized **"Satyagraha,"** the policy of non-violent resistance initiated by the Great Ghandi.

In 1954 Dr. King excepted his first pastorate at the Dexter Avenue Baptist Church in Montgomery, Alabama; a church consisting of a well educated congregation that had been recently led by Reverend Vernon Johns, a strong principled Black man, and great Church pastor who was an aggressive leader who challenged segregation and was thought to be "too" aggressive for the "conservative" membership of the Church. Bless the name of the Lord Jesus Christ; because change was destined to come. On December 1, 1955, Rosa Parks, an upstanding Negro woman, was arrested and put in jail after refusing to move to the back of the transit bus for a white person as required by a racist segregationist law. A meeting of the Negro leadership was assembled to address the issue.

A new organization and concept was formulated; the organization was called the Montgomery Improvement Association (M. I. A.) and Dr. Martin Luther King Jr. was elected President. The treatment and imprisonment of Rosa Parks was the final straw and the catalyst for the change to come. Negroes in Montgomery, Alabama rallied, organized, and in December of 1955, 42,000 strong; these Negroes began on a truly great endeavour. They embarked on a boycott of Montgomery City buses to protest racially segregated seating. Following 381 days of carpooling, taking cabs, and walking the hostile streets of Montgomery, righteousness won, fairness won; equality obtained the victory. Negroes successfully obtained their right to desegregate seating on public buses; a right naturally due.

This victory was very significant both in nature and scope. It was specifically important for the Negroes of Montgomery, Alabama; the Negro could once again ride the bus, but now with dignity and equality. It was significant in larger terms of Negro America; for the Negro witnessed the revealing and implementation of focused collective power. A willingness of a people to unite and agree individually to do what ever it takes to contribute their part in achieving the larger goal. Dr. Martin Luther King Jr. was here it to facilitate change. History teaches us that change is normally facilitated by violence; murder, Coup de' ta, invasion, assassination, or war. Dr. Martin Luther King Jr. was able to facilitate without any of the aforementioned. In 1957 Dr. King helped found the Southern Christian Leadership Conference (SCLC), an organization consisting of African American ministers and Churches focused on challenging racial segregation and utilized nonviolent action such as marches, boycotts, and demonstrations. Dr. King made many strategic alliances; Black, White, Jewish, etc. and began to influence public opinion in the United States. In 1959 Dr. King visited India to obtain a detailed understanding of **satyagraha**, Gandhi's principle of non-violent persuasion, which Dr. King wanted to engage as the instrument to pursue social change in America. In 1960 Dr. King gave up his pastorate at Dexter Avenue Baptist Church in Montgomery, Alabama to become Co-Pastor with his father, of Ebenezer Baptist Church in Atlanta, Georgia.

Dr. King's work and sacrifice resulted in being the key instrument in the passing of the Civil Rights Acts of 1964, which prohibited segregation in public accommodations as well as discrimination in education and employment. For this and his moral stance and effective non-violent persuasion and awakening or giving the United States and the world a consciousness for fairness, he was awarded the 1964 Noble Prize for Peace. It resulted in the passing of the Voting Rights Act of 1965, signed by President Lyndon Baines Johnson, which suspended the use of literacy test and other voter qualification test that were being used to prevent Negroes from registering to vote, which were followed by Amendments that banned it. The methodology of Dr. Martin Luther King, Jr. for progress, despite its' success, was questioned by The Honorable El-Hajj Malik El-Shabazz; known to most as Malcolm X. A gifted, focused, and among the most influential Black leaders since the arrival of Africans to the Americas. Malcolm X believed and advocated self-reliance, dignity, and the right of Blacks to defend themselves against unwarranted violent attacks they often endured without recourse. However, understand that Malcolm X's disagreement with Martin Luther King, Jr. was in nature, not in scope. Malcolm questioned the method, not the mission.

A PEOPLE ON A MISSION

The work and presence of Malcolm X is quite important in the struggle for progress and equality in the United States of America and gave birth to a new focus and movement. Malcolm's life was one which consisted of love; grounded in righteousness, tragedy, pain, political consciousness, triumph, and sacrifice. A life which provides a fantastic example of the metamorphosis and evolution of a man spiritually guided to make a difference. His evolution to true political and religious consciousness and the sharing of these truths' and knowledge, to really address the issue, resulted in his assassination. To silence of the true issue; Economics.

The Autobiography of Malcolm X is a, "must read" for anyone, regardless of race, creed or color; seeking to understand the personal development of a leader; a true, righteous leader. I especially request our children in schools and college students of all races and cultures in all universities worldwide. It will teach them that greatness does not discriminate nor is confined to a person or race of people or a class of people; for greatness stands alone through deeds and contributions which help others and then stands as a lighthouse or beacon for others to be inspired and motivated to strive to obtain an understanding of the political realities at hand and the obtaining political consciousness, and using it for success. Malcolm's life and contribution to Black America is a great and above reproach; ironically Malcolm X has had a greater impact for America and Black American politics and culture dead then alive. Malcolm X gave birth to the Black Panther Party, founded by Huey Newton and Bobby Seale in Oakland, California in October 1966; which focused on self-defense, self-reliance and restructuring American society to make it more politically, socially, and economically equal.

Labeled as a Militant Black Political organization originally known as the Black Panther Party for Self-Defense, the Black Panthers made a strong and positive impact on Black America, which presented a problem for the powers that be, White America. Contrary to the propaganda submitted, the Black Panthers were not initiators of violence nor were they radical. They simply advocated self-reliance and self-defense and defended the rights of Blacks to defend themselves in their communities against unwarranted police attacks and brutality. They promoted the development of strong Black led and controlled Institutions and Organizations. They called for Black people to work together to protect their rights and to improve their economic and social conditions. They welcomed alliances with White activists such as the Students for a Democratic Society and the Weather Underground, because they believed that revolutionaries who wanted to change American society should work together across racial lines. They developed and implemented programs which provided free breakfast for children, established free medical clinics, assisted the homeless in finding housing, and gave free clothing and food to the poorest in the community. A Militant Black Political organization; hardly.

The uncompromised dedication and focus of the Honorable El-Hajj Malik El-Shabazz (Malcolm X) and his message made a quite notable impact on the Civil Rights Movement from his release from prison and greatly in the last year of his life. Black Activists in an organization called the Congress Of Racial Equality (C. O. R. E.), originators of the Freedom Rides; and another organization called the Student Non-Violent Coordinating Committee (SNCC) led by Stokely Carmichael; another of the few politically consciousness Black men of the time. Stokely; a strong and focused leader, changed his name in 1978 to Kwame Toure'; taking the first name of his mentor Kwame Nkrumah of Ghana and the last name of Ahmed Sekdu Toure' of Guinea. They heard Malcolm X speak to organizers in Selma, Alabama in February of 1965 and began to listen to, and of more importance, heard and began to understand the message of Malcolm X and reason for the mission of Malcolm X and his constant Eye on the Prize and his advocation for self-defense, self-reliance, racial pride, and the creation of Black Organizations and Institutions operated and controlled by Blacks. Stokely Carmichael gave it a name "Black Power."

* * *

CHAPTER VII

A MOVEMENT MISUNDERSTOOD

The Black Power Movement was one of both success and failure; of both achievement and acquiescence; and one of the utmost importance in the anthology of the Negro in the United States of America. The very basic platform of the Black Power Movement was distorted in order to influence the perception of the general public, both Black and White; by the powers that be. They created the perception of the movement as a movement advocating racial divisions, rejecting coalitions with white people and white organizations, being defeatist, and bitterly rejecting the Civil Rights Movement's goal of integration and equality. This is despite the fact that many explanations in interviews and conferences provided focused on the denial of these charges and branding; in an attempted and pushed to move discussions forward to talk about the real concept of Black Power and the movement in terms of its importance in pluralistic American politics and society. Think about it; every other race in America possesses some racial power; and the political, economic, and social power which follows or accompanies it.

The Black Power Movement was not a call for anti-white perspectives and racial isolation. Nor was it a call for violence and revolution. It was simply a call for self-help. It was a call for racial pride and progress. It was a legitimate acknowledgment of the historically chronicled fact that for any group, be it racial, social, geographic, or economic or ethnic; in order to become a respected, effective, and progressive participant in American society and the American political system, cohesive organization was vital. Every other group in America has embraced this and excelled because they did not overlook or required a reminder of this vital factor. What is interesting is that when Blacks began to apply this lesson to themselves, they were branded as "radicals", "separatist" who wanted "to go against the grain," as it were.

The misrepresentation of Black Power and its true meaning and purpose created many differing interpretations of its purpose, and with it, a turbulent milieu. Liberal's, Conservatives, and advocates could see that Black Power was a call for self-determination and, to use a conservative term, "pulling up themselves by their bootstraps." Some interpreted it as a legitimate call for cohesive organization. Many conservatives and liberals, both black and white, saw it as the pursuit of Black Capitalism. Some interpreted it as a call for a separate nation; linking Black Power to Malcolm X's early 1960's speeches which propelled the Nation of Islam in its call for a distinct Black Nation. These were the political interpretations. The social interpretations were mixed. Social and political interpretations often relate. The question was and the question continues to possess relevance today," *is equality achieved through marching for government intervention to grant and enforce "equal treatment", the answer or to unite to uplift and elevate ourselves by simply working together."* Just like every other race of people.

Cultural interpretations were progressive, interesting; yet provocative. Many felt that specific attention to "The Black Experience" and the crippling effect of the Institution of Slavery upon Black people needed to be acknowledged and the accompanying loss of Black history; which was African history in culture. This sparked defensive style political reaction by larger society, to downplay the acknowledgment. However, within this process, a cultural phenomenon began. The attention to the Black Experience resulted in a cultural recognition and appreciation by Black people; the changing of names, changing of the hair styles to afros, change of fashion to the dashikis, changing the style of the names of children from Ann, Robert, and Mary to Dameka, Jamal, and Salequa, changing the way in which Negroes wanted to be officially acknowledged; from Negro to Black. These are the actions of a people seeking their roots and history and desiring to find their identity in a vastly pluralistic society called America. Clearly cohesive organization (consciously or unconsciously) and reaction took place in this component. Organizations and Associations led by Blacks developed, such as the Congressional Black Caucus, formed in 1970. A black consciousness was indeed taking place in the urban centers and communities of America; however, not collectively. We did not move the plans and works of neither Reverend Dr. Martin Luther King, Jr. or Malcolm X forward. We merely rested on their work.

A MOVEMENT MISUNDERSTOOD

The larger society began to move towards a *race per se* atmosphere which politicized other groups such as Latinos, Chinese, and other ethnic groups, Women, the Handicapped, and shortly thereafter, Gays and Lesbians. Everyone started to comprehend the benefits of uniting on the basis of identity. This diluted the call for Black Power. "Better to just let sleeping dogs lie," many stressed, let's not focus on race, oppression, or economics; we have been promised Inclusion. Inclusion in all of the factors of American life; social, corporate, educational, and political. Inclusion in the decision making process, access to power. Did we get it? Do we have power? What is the Black definition of power? Blacks are allowed in venues, associations, offices, and positions as never before. There are over 10,000 Black elected officials throughout the United States at present; members of the United States Congress, Mayors, Members of City and County Councils, School Board Members, State and local Delegates and legislators, and members of the United States Senate. Blacks head local police departments, and hold many policy making positions which involve the allocation of resources and capital to whom, for what, and when. However, do we have power? Black visibility is not Black Power.

Blacks indeed have a strong presence in America and in American society. Blacks are attending schools in every educational level and area of study, enjoy a greater presence in corporate America, in law firms, in professional sports, television, music, and entertainment; making millions of dollars. Yet, simultaneously, Blacks continue to have a disproportionate presence in the negative areas of American life. Right now, they are more black males in prison than in college; Blacks are disproportionately residing in sub-standard housing; Blacks are more likely to be a victim of violent crime; disproportionately unemployed, and disproportionately without health insurance. Ironically, many of the people referenced above making millions of dollars came from the environments and circumstances also referenced above. Black presence is not Black Power.

Perhaps the problem lies in the fundamental understanding of what is Black Power. Black Power not being the only Black in the company and relishing in that; Black Power is using your position and work performance to excel, and then to help get the second black and third Black hired. Black Power is not using the Church as a way of obtaining and building wealth for the Pastor on Sunday while the surrounding community and his people suffer every day; Black Power is in using the Church as a power base to inspire and help the people to help each other, and using the Church's wealth and resources to help the community and empower the community to help itself. Black Power is not Black politicians being served by the people, Black Power lies in serving; enacting legislation that is "truly" in the best interest of the people thereby helping to address the needs of the people.

Black Power is Jim Brown. A member of the College Hall of Fame in Football and Lacrosse, member of the National Football League Hall of Fame, successful actor, activist, *Free Man*. The Honorable Jim Brown personifies the utilization of one's success, presence, and influence to motivate, represent, and assist Black people and communities to be able to help themselves and each other. He utilized his fame and credibility to obtain the trust of the two most dangerous gangs in the United States; leveraged that trust and brought them together and personally negotiated a Peace Agreement. Jim Brown brought the leadership of the Bloods and the leadership of the Crips to his estate and they remained at the stately manor until they reached the high ground of understanding and mutual agreement in the holy ground of love for one another and for peace. Sponsoring mentoring programs, addressing youth and community issues, challenging other famed black athletes, actors, and entertainers to utilize their success and presence to inspire, to reach out to the youth and the community, show some sort of interest, sponsor something; speak to issues of importance to the Black community, at least when asked.

Black Power is The Honorable Thurgood Marshall. The first Black United States Solicitor General, and the first Black Supreme Court Justice, and the most successful attorney to ever argue before the United States Supreme Court, bringing 32 cases before the Supreme Court, and winning 29 of them. The most noted and of most significance is the case of *Brown vs. Board of Education* (1954) which outlawed segregation in American public life; toppling the Supreme Court's ruling in *Plessy vs. Ferguson* (1896) and it's "separate but equal" formula. Marshall argued that the mere fact of racial separation, even without the gross inequality, the irrevocably harmed Black American children. The court unanimously agreed. As a judge for the U. S. Court of Appeals, position to which President John F. Kennedy appointed him in 1961, of the 112 opinions he wrote for that court, not one was overturned on appeal. As a Supreme Court Justice Marshall continued to stand for righteousness. Known as the "great dissenter," Marshall stood firmly for the rights of poor people and minorities and against the death penalty even as the court grew more conservative in the 1980's. Thurgood Marshall did not allow his personal and professional success to change him nor his overall mission. He leveraged his presence and power to give us power.

Black Power is Paul Robeson; dramatic actor, singer of spirituals, Civil Rights activist and visionary, and to many; a political radical. Paul Robeson was one of the most gifted men of the 1900's. His resonant bass and commanding presence made him a world-renowned singer and actor of both film and stage. Long before the **"Black Power Movement,"** he stressed the importance of the Negro of being proud to be Black....."For no one respects a man who does not respect himself." Robeson used his fame and success as a platform to bring attention to issues and advocate for fairness and Negro empowerment. Robeson said that it was imperative for the Negro to regain and appreciate their African roots. He endured pressures and professional losses for his strength; in the 1930's, 1940's, 1950's; to make a stand. He supported important righteous political causes world-wide. He could have easily rested on his great abilities and *"coast"* on those great abilities and the accompanying fame and said nothing; and did nothing.

Black Power is Maynard Jackson Jr., three-time mayor of Atlanta, Georgia; who propelled the city to be the most prominent Black City in the United States. At age 34, Maymard Jackson was not only Atlanta's first Black Mayor, but also its' youngest. He served the people in the community and the business community by creating an atmosphere and metropolitan area where everyone excelled; a business friendly environment which attracted businesses and corporations which helped the city, the community and the citizens therein. Within his third term, Atlanta was the host city of the 1992 Democratic National Convention and Jackson further marketed the progressive image and vibrant corporate life, and International appeal of Atlanta to impress the International Olympic Committee which brought the 1996 Olympic Games to Atlanta. At the same time, he made sure that the people of Atlanta benefited as well. Jobs, business opportunities, housing, schools, teachers, community building and empowerment. Maynard Jackson Jr. did not take his Eye off the Prize even after possessing individual and political power; he used his presence, commitment, and Power to inspire and equip the people to help themselves.

Black Power is Dr. Benjamin L. Hooks, Lawyer, Judge, Reverend, Civil Rights leader, humanitarian. The Honorable Dr. Hooks utilized his skills, accomplishments, presence and power to facilitate progress for African Americans. The first African American to become a Criminal Court Judge in the State of Tennessee, the first African American to sit on the Federal Trade Commission, former Executive Director of the NAACP, first African American to address both the Democratic National Convention and Republican National Conventions, respected leader. Meeting, spending time with, and becoming friends with this icon is a great blessing for me. The knowledge of what happened in the 1940's, 1950's, 1960's, in Memphis, in Mississippi, in Alabama, the struggle, the movement and his insight on the events, and why, and what should be happening now; brought to tears to eyes. He continues to advocate, speak, to teach, and fight. Commitment above reproach.

Black Power is The Honorable Ossie Davis; world-renowned actor, playwright, producer, director, humanitarian, political activist, free man, in fact, **A Man Among Men**. A pillar in the Black Power Movement, Civil Rights Movement, the Cultural Revolution, Ossie provided interpretations of the political and social issues of the time despite the cost. He endured being black-listed (black-balled in present terms), for taking a stand. Friend and strong supporter of the father of Political Consciousness and the Black Power Movement; Malcolm X, and the father of Social Consciousness and Fairness; Dr. Martin Luther King, Jr. He implemented power. Black Power is The Honorable Ruby Dee; superstar actress, writer, social activist, wife of Ossie Davis, a free woman. Greatly leveraged and jeopardized her career, success, and life for her heart and willingness to stand up. She successfully interprets, portrays and communicates messages of political and social consciousness vital to the growth and progress of Black America and understanding to all of America.

Black Power is the Reverend Jesse Jackson; a constant advocate for Civil Rights, economic justice, and racial equality. Although criticized, Jesse Jackson has worked to assist, inspire, and empower African Americans and others races and is not afraid to speak out on issues of exclusion and other inequities while others stand by. Black Power is Marion Barry; like it or not, like him or not; recognize or not, accomplished a great deal as a fighter for civil rights and equality, and as Mayor of Washington, DC helped countless numbers of citizens and youth by creating job training and employment; made many African American businesses and business people wealthy by providing equal access to contracts, and forced the large corporations doing business with District of Columbia to promote and hire qualified Blacks.

Perhaps the problem is not one of fundamental understanding; but one of consciousness. Consciousness is defined as having an awareness of one's own existence, sensations, and thoughts, and of one's environment. This could be the problem indeed. Are African Americans truly conscious? Is there a true awareness of **who** we are; **where** we are as a race of people; **why** we are where we are? Are we learning from history? Do we even know the importance of history? History is down-played in this pluralistic society of America. History has a bad reputation and too often looked upon by too many people as essentially a series of events and the dates on which they occurred. I grow weary when people say or ask: why study history? Why study this or that particular date or these events and what followed? What does that have to do with today? Everything. Your knowledge of where you have been teaches you make better decisions now and have better insight on where you should be going.

A MOVEMENT MISUNDERSTOOD

My father, The Honorable William P. Parker Gatling told me when I was eight years old, **"Son, know everything you can; learn and understand everything you can; knowledge is a key and a weapon that can not be taken from you. Know History son, know your history as well as the history of other races and cultures, History provides knowledge and insight."** Although my father died when I was 12 years old on Saturday morning between 8:30 a.m. and 9:00 a.m. (he told me awake him at 9:00 a.m.), five days before Thanksgiving 1974 at the age of 48; his wisdom and teachings through his life experiences and of the knowledge his father passed to him from the knowledge he received for my great grandfather and mother in their parents that he passed to me. He empowered me with my history of then he charged me with a mission which I strangely understood to the point that when he died, he had prepared me. I was a 12 year old man. Blessed with my mother Naomi Gatling who knew that I was charged with the mission by my father and trusted in me to me the right decisions together with the love and respect of God.

We must connect our children to their history. To their family history and forefathers in America at a minimum, to their history and culture from Africa, and of the many contributions to the dominance of the United States globally. Black history should not be of interest or of importance merely in February because it is the designated month for "Black History." Cultural and family history should be within the knowledge set of Black children as in other races. It is the knowledge of history and learning from the lessons it provides that enables one to make better decisions because one has information of past events, outcomes, and experiences that where passed on. It should be passed as lessons and points of reference and instruments to engage, enlighten, and charge our children and youth within a responsibility to strive for education, progress, and success; constantly coupled with God. In fact, it is this passing on the Black history of oppression, toil, sacrifice, contribution, and success in the United States of America in spite of the prevailing times, century, era, or decade, and the lessons that lie therein, that the African American community, the leadership, youth, and children are not getting. Yet, it is greatly needed. It appears that Black History is to be celebrated (in the 2nd month of calender year); but not be studied or learned from.

Believe it or not, everything we do is in some way related to and influenced by History. The things we do, the things we say, the way we live, the way we worship, or not; even the things we will do; regardless of race, religion, color, class, or culture; is influenced by History. It's importance cannot be dismissed. History embodies the essence of knowledge. Blacks are the only race of people in which their decisions and actions do not reflect a comprehensive learning from History.

We sing songs, hold Marches, have parades, and light candles to commemorate Black History; yet, do not utilize its teachings in our goal setting and decision making. In fact, the very songs we sing find their basis in History, in Slavery, and in Negro life in the United States of America.

First there is Gospel music. The multi-billion dollar gospel music industry of today, the "recording artist", choirs, quartets, singers and the songs that they sing, is rooted in Negro Slavery. Planting, cultivating, and harvesting cotton, tobacco, sugar, etc., creating tremendous wealth for America. Day after day, month after month, year after year, decade after decade, generation after generation; our great-great-great-great grandfathers and mothers toiled, suffered, sang, and prayed. Yes prayed; the Negro is a very spiritual being, although not as much now.

One of the most common forms of religious expression were *"spirituals"*, many serving a double purpose. Slave masters often encouraged the music because they saw the spirituals as simple hymns and thought that singing Slaves were happy Slaves. However, these hymns often facilitated a vital role in teaching the Bible to slaves who were not literate, because the lyrics of common spirituals re-communicated the narrative story of the Bible from Genesis to Revelation. And many songs and the lyrics therein maintained secret meanings. For example, it was common knowledge among the Slaves who sang spirituals such as "I Am Bound for the Promised Land" did not only refer to Heaven, and the great song "Steal Away" did not only refer to Jesus. Spirituals provided a method of covertly communicating plans and directions for escape from the plantation. It is for these reasons that spirituals and Slave Religion played an irreplaceable part of Slave life. It provided the basis for at least some sort of a cohesive community in which Slaves were able to communicate more openly and express themselves more freely than in any other way, shape, or form. Through this community, with its' shared experiences, rituals, beliefs, and songs; Slaves were able to find spiritual validation and hope for the future. These songs and rituals were the main components of "Slave Religion", which is now none as the Black Church.

Slave Religion is the religious beliefs and practices of Negro Slaves, specifically in North America. In a system in which housing, food, clothing, employment, mobility, and even marriage were all regulated by slave owners; Religion was the only form of slave expression not completely under white control. Many slave owners allowed the "Religious meetings", as called, for they believed that Christian slaves would be more docile. They were seeking more Negro adherence to a verse in the Bible stating "Slaves, obey your masters." However, as the slaves learned more about the Bible they were intrigued and then empowered by reading, interpreting, and receiving the messages that the Bible held for them. Other slave owners did not allow their slaves to attend the religious meetings because they felt threatened by such communal gatherings or they did not believe that Slaves even possessed souls to be saved.

Religious meetings provided important ritual and communal opportunities for the Negroes brought to North America by force, to collectively connect and worship. Opportunities to connect to their history and traditions, while simultaneously, creating an adjusted belief system which was needed to adapt to a new way of life in a New World. Slave congregations became new versions of traditional African village, with the Slave Preacher serving as a leader, facilitator, advocate. Preachers, Pastors, and Members of the Clergy please make note of the true job which accompanies your **"Calling"**, as it were. Not personal prosperity, power, and being served; but Community prosperity, empowerment, and serving. Spirituals and hymns evolved into Gospel music in the Post Reconstruction Era and greatly influenced the Blues.

The Blues is a uniquely Black American musical form which reflects the times and particular history and culture of Black America. It emerged during the troubled times of the Post Reconstruction South, when Southern Blacks experienced political disfranchisement, economic subordination, social disregard, and violence. Random, unjustified, heartless, and systematic physical violence. There's no true way to determine when the Blues first appeared officially. History reveals that is also rooted in Slavery. History relates its origin in Slavery in to forms; *Field Hollers* and *Ballards*. Field hollers were work songs, generally extemporized an unaccompanied, which evolved from the "call and response" work songs that would set the pace for group labor on Antebellum Slave Plantations. In the early 20th Century the Blues moved from the American South to the North, accompanying The Great Migration. This brief period of Black American migration to the North is one of great importance in the context of Black history and the history of the United States is of America. The Great Migration brought massive numbers of Southern Blacks to the urban North and West, which presented an insurmountable obstacle to the goals of the Northern Black elite to assimilate into White middle-class religion, music, society and life. The Blues itself shifted from simple rural Blues to rhythmic and rollicking urban Blues. During the 20th century the Blues became the most recognized musical form in the world through it's role in Rhythm and Blues (R & B) and early Rock 'n Roll. It also became an important influence in Jazz.

Jazz is one of the crowning creations and accomplishments of Negro culture.

This 20th century music, characterized by improvisation, a rhythmic conception termed "swing" and the emphasis placed on each musical instrument and musician achieving a uniquely identifiable sound that continues to evolve as it incorporates new musical influences, including Gospel music, Latin American music, European Art music, and Rock-n-Roll. Jazz musicians have consistently challenged musical boundaries and played a major role in challenging Racial discrimination. In 1935 Benny Goodman made Teddy Wilson the pianist in his trio, breaking the Color Barrier. He shortly thereafter hired Black vibraphonist Lionel Hampton, making his group a quartet. Throughout the late 1930's, The Goodman Quartet was the most prominent interracial Jazz group in the United States. Many Jazz greats followed.

Rap Music emerged from the Hip Hop Movement of New York; particularly in the South Bronx in the 1970's and continues to grow in popularity in America and Internationally. The musical roots of Rap stretch equally far back in history, drawing upon African, Afro Caribbean, and Black American rhythmic styles. In contrast to Western European Music; which emphasizes harmonic progression and a sense of linear, forward motion, African music often designates time, emphasizes cycles, incorporates poly rhythmic figures, and includes non-harmonic percussive sounds. Rap Music originally took his rhythms from the Soul & Funk of James Brown, George Clinton, and a couple others who had emerged from the Rhythm and Blues tradition. Rap Music was catapulted into the public eye in the fall of 1979 when a group of Rappers from Brooklyn, New York called **The Sugar Hill Gang** released the hit single *"Rapper's Delight."* Much to dismay of the brothers from the Bronx, the song topped on the charts and reached number 36 or the Billboard's Top 40. This was followed in 1980 by a Rapper named Kurtis Blow who scored two hit singles, *"Christmas Rappin"* and *"The Breaks,"* both of which went Gold. Rap Music was here, and here to stay.

As the Rap musical form developed and achieved popularity, other types and styles of Rap music and Rapping were introduced. The popularity accompanied by huge record sales gave birth to his commercialization and by the mid 1980's Rap and Rap styled music had become part of the mainstream of America. And at the same time gave birth to a new culture. Rap is presently the most recognized musical form in the world. It is the most often used musical form in TV and Radio Commercials, Movie Soundtracks, even in theme songs of TV shows, including a popular Police TV show "Cops", despite the fact the Rap music and Rappers voice nothing but disrespect and hatred for the Police because of their traditional treatment of Black people.

A MOVEMENT MISUNDERSTOOD

Rap music was created as a homemade Community-based musical form, expanded by commercialization; however, commercialization did not steal it from the streets. In fact, the commercialization of Rap into mainstream America intensified its persona and affect on the children and youth in the urban communities and suburbs of America. Further, Rap music has produced a culture far larger in scope than envisioned. A "Rap Culture", which has developed and grown and has become larger then the Industry itself. The genie is out of the bottle.

Rap music and the culture that it has created is truly a situation where Life has imitated Art. We must be very careful with Rap music and the messages expressed and displayed, the attitude and culture that it has created among an entire generation, because its impact on the children is tremendous. However there are bigger fish to fry at this present time. Everything in life and everyone exists in cycles. It is at the core of evolution. It is at the core of all life and its stages. We are now in a new millennium and about to engage in another cycle or cycles; if you will, and must be prepared. We are about to take part in a generational cycle, an economic, political, and social cycle that we are not prepared for. What started as a Movement for Black people; the pursuit of *Equal Treatment [Non-Violently] and Black Power [Non-Violently]*; **Collective Power;** cohesive organization; has now become; not evolved, into the pursuit of power for Me. The pursuit of power for Me; not for We.

* * *

CHAPTER VIII

THE TASK AT HAND

In 1975, the National Urban League, under the brilliant, focused and innovative leadership of Vernon Jordan, began issuing an annual report called, *The State of Black America*, which speaks to the situation, status and progress or lack of progress of Blacks in the United States of America. Black America is currently in **A State of Emergency**. Black on Black crime and violence, record highs of Black Males in jail while record lows in college enrollment, the ungodly disrespect of the Black Woman, the shameful lack of integrity of Black Politicians, and the disregard of our obligation to the children. Rap Music, the industry, its' commercialization, the messages, behavior, and attitudes they convey have influenced and dominated an entire generation and if Rap Music continues to go unchecked will cause great and perhaps irreparable damage. The advocation and celebration of robbery, drug-dealing, and violence that the children see in music videos and listen to on compact disc hailing the life of the Thug. Our tragic collective ignorance of the importance and outright necessity of educating and inspiring the children and the youth. Finally and perhaps of most significance; being unprepared for this new millennium of economics, politics, and technologies.

The United States economy will endure a major recession in five to eight years from now to due the change in generation cycles and in the change in spending which accompanies the change. Every 40 years, a new generation is formed through birth and immigration. This has been tracked as far back as the 1400's and in extensive academic detail in two books: *Generations* (Morrow, 1992) and *The Fourth Turning* (Broadway, 1997), both written by William Strauss and Neil Howe. However, within this generational cycle lies spending cycles which provide indicators and insight on the economy. The recession will be due to the natural shift in economic cycles; the reduction and end of spending by the Baby-Boomer Generation which has moved and facilitated the growth and expansion of the United States economy for almost half a century.

The Baby-Boomers have moved the stock market, companies, and industries. When the Baby-Boomers were babies Gerber Baby Food stock boomed, in their youth Schwinn Bike Company stock boomed, created and expanded technology in their prime (Microsoft, Intel, Dell), created the constantly booming Weight-Loss industry and Exercise industry to stay fit, and now the boom in plastic surgery and other surgical procedures to look fit. The Baby-Boomer generation are in their peak spending years now and will begin to decline in 2009. This will induce a major economic shift; on both the Macro and Micro level. As an Economist and constant humble student of Economics, I submit to you that America is not prepared for this cyclical shift.

As complex as our economy is in its day-to-day operations, over the long-term it is amazingly predictable. It is predictable for one simple yet paramount reason. Our economy is driven by the family spending cycles of each new generation of consumers and workers. In the short term, there are many factors that affect our economy; Interest Rates rise and fall. Trade deficits expand and contract. The Yen gets stronger, than the Dollar gets stronger, the Dollar gets weaker, the Euro gets stronger, affecting the competitiveness of our multi-national companies in foreign markets. The one fundamental factor that drives the Boom and Bust cycles of the United States economy overtime in a predictable manner is not a matter of politics, interest rates, trade deficits or the strength of the Dollar. It is consumption. Consumption and spending behavior and patterns over time. Spending and consumption drive economies.

When I prayed to God for permission and guidance to dare to engage the task at hand for Black America in specific terms and to engage all of America, I asked the Heavenly Father to allow me to study, learn, and communicate the truth. There are many issues to address in the general context of Black America, however, we will deal with the tasks specifically because solving the specific problems will dissolve the general ones.

Economics

Economics is the key factor in any nation, state, or community. There is power in Economics. Consumer spending is the key component in economics and its cycles. Blacks control a considerable spending dollar which tends to be spent quickly and without consciousness or prioritizing. Blacks America earns and controls $631 Billion ($631,000,000,000.00) in income per year, but the spending patterns are questionable to state it politely. The National Urban League's *"State of Black America 2004"* report found that fewer than 50% of Black families owned their own homes as compared with more than 70% of Whites. While 79% of Whites invest in the stock market, only 61% of Black Americans do.

So where does the core problem exist? Spending priorities. Black Americans tend to spend a significant amount of their earned income on depreciable products. In 2002, a year of suffering for the United States economy, mainly due to the terrorist attack of September 11, 2001 on the World Trade Center, Blacks spent $22.9 Billion ($22,900,000,000.00) on clothes, $3.2 Billion ($3,200,000,000.00) on electronics and $11.6 Billion ($11,600,000,000.00) on furniture to put into homes that, in many cases, were rented. There is considerable spending on cars and liquor. Blacks make up only 12% of the total United States population, yet account for 30% of the country's Scotch consumption. We must evaluate spending and spending decisions with consideration to *Wants vs. Needs*.

The only area where Blacks are appearing to be "cutting-back," as it where, is in spending on Books. **Books!** Total Book purchases have tragically gone from a high of $356 Million In 2000 to $303 Million in 2002. The Ariel Mutual Funds/Charles Schwab's 2003 Black Investor Survey found that when comparing households where Blacks and Whites had roughly the same household incomes; whites saved nearly 20% more each month for retirement; and of Blacks earning $100,000 a year had less than $5,000 in retirement savings than Whites. This short-sighted behavior must be acknowledged and addressed.

Power lies within Economics. Power lies with spending and spending choices and priorities. Black America has Economic Power. Its strongest weapon as a Race of People in The United States of America in terms of presenting an ability to make a statement; Economically, Politically, or Socially. The problem; not issue, for we have developed a habit of utilizing the term "issues" to replace the truth and the true explanative; **"problems,"** is that we do not acknowledge this power. We are too busy engaging in pursuits of social acceptance and personal gratification to engage the serious task at hand of progress and building a future for the children.

Black America must look at its consumption. The basis of spending and consumption is need. Consumer spending should always be a factor of need; not a desire, for which one uses to rationalize spending. We must plan and look to the future. If you cannot see yourself ten years from now; by God please be able to at least see yourself ten months from now. Savings and investing must become part of our knowledge set. We must establish spending priorities. A penny saved is truly a penny earned. Pay yourself one penny for every ten pennies you earn. We must engage the Hierarchy of Needs as opposed to the short-sightedness of the Pursuit of Wants. We must cease the *"Keeping up with the Jones's"* and focus on keeping up with the pace of the economy, the innovations, the technologies, and politics of America as they change and as they relate to Black America and *The State of Black America.*

Education

Knowledge is the cornerstone of evolution. It is the ultimate tool. It is knowledge and the application of knowledge that has provided America the technological advances, cures for diseases, economic, political, and military power over another nations. Knowledge, which is powered by Education, is a means of power. Our pursuit of wealth and fame is tremendous, our pursuit of fun and sex is outrageous, but our pursuit for education is dismal. Our respect for and our emphasis on education has diminished. There is no progress, no evolution without Education. Our diminished respect for education has resulted in our collective stagnation. There is a lack of emphasis on education in the Black community.

It is important that we remember that without education it is difficult to develop the consciousness, the social skills, and knowledge necessary for our youth and children to be masters of their own destinies. Education must become a priority. Educating the children is just as much a parental duty as feeding and clothing them. Allow me to submit this question; How many Jewish American, Asian American, or Arab American Professional Baseball, Basketball, or Football Players or Singers do you know of? Some would preface their response with arguments on natural differences. This is not totally accurate. Conversely; How many Jewish American, Asian American, or Arab American Doctors, Lawyers, Judges, Scientists, or Business Owners do you know of?

I submit to you that this is primarily because of cultural priorities engaged and pursued by these groups of Americans. Education is a priority. Knowledge and awareness of their History and the persons, places, and events that make up their history. The children are taught and groomed early to take school and education seriously and to have strong academic interests and pursuits. This is precisely what the Black American Community must do. We must make school and education a priority for our children.

A High Diploma should be expected and demanded of all Black children from their parents and relatives. Followed by college and post-graduate pursuits whenever possible. Over the past several years there have been several corporations, companies, and organizations that have donated significant funds for scholarships for Blacks; however, a significant sum of the funds get returned due to A LACK OF INTEREST.

We must recognize and embrace the importance of Education and History for our children. With this knowledge our children and youth will have an awareness of their heritage and identity, and then begin to develop a dedicated passion to achieve and maintain conscious, thoughtful, voluntary self-control; their ability to first love themselves; to maintain respectful relations and positive regard among themselves and others. To engage, act, and demonstrate ways of thinking and relating which expand their consciousness and behavioral repertoire.

Watch The P's: Priest, Pastors, Politicians

Once upon a time, certain positions and occupations had a degree of honor, of integrity, of righteousness. These were once positions utilized to serve and to help the people and held by individuals who wanted to help and to serve. Not to be served. Now these positions are utilized as platforms for obtaining personal pleasure, power, and prosperity. The P's have violated and disrespected the ethical responsibilities which accompany these sworn positions. Further, they have violated the trust, the adherence, and the respect of the very people they took an oath to inspire, enlighten, serve and represent.

Abuses of our trust in the Church and abuses of our children by Priests being revealed. Preachers and Pastors using the Church and the paramount importance of God in the existence and maintaining of Mankind as a means for serving their egos, their bank accounts, and their libidos. I submit to you that many of them do not truly believe in God. True Clergy takes the humble honor of being called by the Truly Magnificent Heavenly Father to serve and give understanding to God's word, God's Love, and God's presence in all factors of life and death. JESUS CHRIST is the model. He never sought prosperity. His concepts called for wealthy to donate that prosperity to the poor. The Pastors must empower their congregations with the Power of God's Word and Presence and inspire them the righteousness to share God's Word and Power with their fellow man. The Pastors are presently using the Church as a business operation. As a cash-cow. Church prosperity should invested in the community, not Merrill Lynch.

Politicians are among the most dangerous of the P's. They should not be believed, trusted, or supported without evaluation. They must be watched. They should be politically audited on an annual basis. Our methods of selecting and supporting them demand adjustment. A few of them honestly enter politics to make a difference. Most enter to make a profit. We must support and elect sincere People, not politicians and have more interest in politics and legislation. When must engage in more serious evaluation of elected officials, their voting and interest. Be not only concerned with a politicians reputation, but with their representation.

Black America must address and adjust its thinking and priorities. Stop blaming the *White Man* for all the problems and madness in our schools, communities, and lives. The Black community must examine itself and see to what degree it has contributed to its own madness, detriment, and stagnation. We must take responsibility for that part of our personality, that part of our behavior, that part of our community, and that part of ourselves over which we have control, and change that part. There are indeed disparities, prejudice, and power-plays that exists, however there are more opportunities now then ever. It is important that we be aware of them and engage and utilize them.

The Black Man is the key factor in the state and future of Black America. He must assert himself. He must learn to love and respect himself more than money or sexual conquest. He must accept responsibility. He must learn to appreciate, respect, and celebrate the Black Woman and her love, beauty, support, and strength. He must be a father to his children. Child Support payments are not Child Support. Black children and youth have been out of control because the Black Man has been missing in action. Forcing single mothers and often grandparents to raise children with great stress and strain. The past negative relationships with Black men often damage the woman's perception of a Real Man and what he represents. This often damages or ends what could be great long-lasting relationships and potential marriages with Men of Honor. They are scared by the deep wounds of past disingenuous men.

The Black Woman continues to be the vital organ of the Black community. She has been forced to single-handedly birth and raise many of the children. She has been used, abused and often abandoned by the Black Man. Black Men have the nerve to be mad about, and sometimes abusive for their sub-conscious, yet and often conscious resentment of the professional, political, and economic success of the Black Woman. She must love herself more than popularity. I endeavour to inspire and celebrate the Black Woman by telling her that she is vital. She is indispensable. She has the utmost right to be concerned about the number of successful, high-profile Black Men getting married to White Women. As a politically conscious Man, of which I am first; and as a Black Man specifically, I support real love in all situations and circumstances regardless of Race, Creed, or Color.

I must emphasize "REAL LOVE."

The Black Man must be sure that his marriage is due to and only due to Real Love. Real, True love, not Economics; not Fame, not Popularity **LOVE;** on the Black Man's part and her part and not due to the Black Man's personal desire to make a statement. One must keep in mind; **One's Desire to make a Statement Today often proves to be a Great Mistake Tomorrow.** Would she be with you if you were not famous or worth $20 Million? Simply endeavour to make sure that you are together because of Love. Not because of the economic and social benefits that she dreamed of.

Our priorities must be evaluated. The children are being ignored and cheated. We are not giving them the love, attention, and inspiration they need and deserve. It is imperative that we emphasize the importance of education to our children and help them whenever possible. Share your time and life experiences with children, this will help them see themselves in the future. Talk with the children. You would be surprised by how much education you give in conversation. I believe with all my heart that with Love and God; we can facilitate change. If we take the time, take an interest in our children we can expand their behavioral orientation and their ability to engage in productive pro-social, proactive activities as opposed to counter-productive, self-defeating and reactionary activities. This must be a priority for all of America; all races and ethnicities.

In Chapter One of this text I talked about the Community of Obedience vs. The Community of Will and the evolution of nations. That once men are broken into obedience, it can be very easily captured and transferred. That a servile community or civilization is a standing invitation to predatory men. However, the Community of Will is an informed, cooperative society of participating wills. It necessitates a synergy of intractable forces. It is difficult to bring about, and yet, more difficult to maintain. The United States of America is the ultimate Community of Will; it has evolved to be the model for individual freedom, opportunity, and success. Further, these are the benefits of an informed, educated, cooperative community, civilization, and nation, *A Nation of Will.*

We now live in a time that man has dreamed of and worked towards for centuries. We now know more than we've ever known. Yet in this Golden Age; within this evolution of knowledge, technology, and information; there should be an evolution of mind, an evolution of consciousness, an evolution of humanity. We have successfully evolved to the *Ideal Community.* A Community of Knowledge and Will. Now that Man has knowledge and free will; he has the opportunity and ability to be righteous. God placed each and every one of us here and now in this time and place for a specific reason. With all this Knowledge and Information abound; our level of love and appreciation for one another and God is sadly low.

We must connect ourselves with God and the Power he provides through faith. It is God and his love and mercy that has sustained us. His power and presence must acknowledged, respected, embraced and passed on. If you think about Man in the context of his relationship with God, you will find Man must be God's favorite creations. Of all living things; of all animals, insects of all species and all scientific or biological classification, Man, *The Human Being* is the only of God's creations that can control and change his surroundings. Man can build, expand, extinguish, develop and destroy, whatever he so chooses. One endeavours to debate this fact will present other species and animals who can build and change its surroundings. Birds build nests. Bees build hives. Ants build colonies and possess their own social organization. However, man can easily displace or destroy them as he builds and expands.

We must be mindful of God's favor for us. He sent his Only Son to the World during a very crucial time to enlighten, empower, and lay down his life for us to live. We must take this to heart and utilize our greatest power; *Love.* We must find the strength to love each other. We must learn to not talk about, at, for, down, and around each other and talk to each other. I believe in the ability of Man. I believe we have a responsibility to God to take care of the children. **To love and respect ourselves and each other.**

THE TASK AT HAND

* * *

Reference

1. George Shepperson, *"Notes on Negro American Influences of the Emergence of African Nationalism,"* Journal of African History, Vol. I No.2, 1960, p. 301

2. H. G. Wells, *The Outline of History,* Vol. II, 1971, Doubleday & Company

3. William Edward Burghardt Du Bois, *Souls of Black Folk,* 1903, Essay and Stretches, Signet Classic

4. Harold Cruse, *Plural But Equal,* New York: Quill-William Morrow, 1987, p. 148

5. William "John" Bryan, *The United States Unresolved Monetary and Political Problems.* Privately Published

6. Frederick Douglass, *Narrative of the Life of Frederick Douglass,* Boston Anti-Slavery Office No. 25, Cornhill, 1845

7. Harriet E. Wilson, *OUR NIG; or Sketches from the Life of a Free Black,* Vintage Books, 1985

8. Kwame Ture and Charles V. Hamilton, *Black Power: The Politics of Liberation,* New York: Random House, 1967

9. Ralph Ellison, *The Invisible Man,* New York: Vintage International, 1947

10. Julius Lester, *To Be A Slave,* New York: Scholastic Inc., 1968

11. Amos N. Wilson, *The Falsification of Afrikan Consciousness,* New York: Afrikan World InfoSystems, 1993

12. Harold J. Berman and William R. Greiner, *The Nature and Functions of the Law,* The Foundation Press Inc., 1958, New York,

13. Harry S. Dent, Jr., *The Roaring 2000's,* Touchstone: Simon and Schuster, 1998

Reference

14. Dr. Benjamin L. Hooks, *The March for Civil Rights,* American Bar Association. 2004

15. Dr. Claud Anderson, *Black Labor/White Wealth, The Search for Power and Economic Justice,* Duncan & Duncan, Inc., 1994

16. Harold Cruse, *The Crisis of the Negro Intellectual,* William Morrow and Company Inc., New York, 1967

17. Gary Allen and Larry Abraham, *None Dare Call It Conspiracy,* Buccaneer Books, Inc., New York, 1976

18. *The Holy Bible,* Old Testament and New Testament, King James Version